Crazy Love

Eileen Leamy

Five Layer Horizon Publishing

~ Contents ~

~ Contents ~

For Jennifer,
who knew me,

For John,
who consoled me,

For Jessamin,
who forgave me,

For Jill,
who loved me already,

and

For Phaedra,
who believed me when
I told her I was going to write this book.

"God isn't angry with you. God is mad for you. God has crazy love for you."

- Father Richard Rohrer
Saints Cyril and Methodius
Byzantine Catholic Church
Cary, North Carolina
October 31, 2010

"I was born to love you."
- Harry

~ Alpha ~

You might think it started with the kiss. You'd be wrong. It didn't even start when I prayed my list. No. It started long before. All those years before we met, we were apart, yet tethered. We were not late-comers to each other's lives; we'd been there all along. The deeper I tunnel back through time, the more I find Harry, smiling in the clouds, shimmering in the stars.

It started at God's drawing board. And who can say when that was?

I married a skeptic. An Eagle Scout who played Mass, Necco wafers for Hosts. A budding scientist set to be a Jesuit until he noticed girls. A faithful husband and father, years deep in Bible studies, prayer groups, weekend marriage encounters... . He would have told you he was devout. And he was.

Until the day his faith failed him, and he turned his back on God.

This is my love story. Although the events I'm going to tell you are mine, this is your love story, too, for one simple reason.

God has crazy love for you.

1

"Do whatever You think."
- Eileen

~ My Prayer ~

Everything starts with, "Yes."

Did you ever have something you just weren't ready to talk to God about? Something you hadn't quite made up your mind about, and you were afraid that if you brought it up with God, He'd run with it? We humans are savvy enough to know how to subtly plant our own ideas into other peoples' minds, so they think they thought of it themselves. The Holy Spirit does that with us. Let's us think something is our idea when it was God's all along. I've come to believe that our reluctance to talk to God is really our unwitting acknowledgment that God already has something in mind for us. We know the train is waiting at the station; we're just not sure we want to get on board.

For several years, I worked at the University of Illinois writing computer based clinical simulations. It was there that I met and married my daughters' father. After a couple years, we went to work at the University of Connecticut to develop clinical simulations to teach obstetricians the new technology of fetal heart rate monitoring during labor. I enjoyed the work immensely, but we were funded through grant money, so when our last grant ran out, we moved to Raleigh, North Carolina to work for IBM. Our jobs were now secure, but our marriage was rocky from the start, and we divorced in 1994. After working as a planner at IBM for 14 years, I went on a pilgrimage and returned resolving to find work I felt had more intrinsic value. So in January, 1999, I started teaching at Wake Technical Community College in Raleigh. The president of the college told me, "If you want an intellectual challenge, go to Chapel Hill (home of the University of North Carolina), but if you want to help turn a life around, this is the place." I loved teaching, loved the students, and felt I was making a real contribution.

So in 2002, I was very happy in the work part of my life. I'd been raising my daughters, Jessamin and Phaedra and contentedly planning to live alone the rest of my life. Over a decade before, a monk at Catholic Social Services had told me the best thing I could do for my daughters was to give them my undivided attention without bringing a man into their lives, at least until they got through high school. I'd already shown I had poor judgment where men were concerned, and I had no desire to run that experiment again. So the monk's advice was actually a great relief to me, and I focused on my work and my daughters for 10 years. I planned that when my youngest daughter, Phaedra, finally left for college, I would fill my life with working, traveling, and learning to play the cello. I had made my plan, and I was content.

For some time, though, a thought had been coming to me more and more, and each time, I pushed it out of my head. But early on a sunny morning the Monday of Holy Week in 2002, I'd dropped my youngest daughter, Phaedra, off at school and was driving to work, when I prayed, in as casual a tone as I could muster, the following prayer:

"Father, I haven't wanted to bring this up with You because I was a little afraid of what You might do, and I want to say I'm perfectly fine living as I am without a man in my life, but I've been thinking that it would be nice to experience what it's like to be married to a man who really knows how to love a person. So what I'm saying is, I can go either way on this. I'm fine as I am,

3

but if You have a different plan in mind, I might be interested in that. And by the way, if You think it's a good idea for me to marry again, I think the man should have certain qualities. He should be someone I can look up to and re-spect. He should have a good sense of humor. He should be a widower with grown children who want him to get married again. He should have had a happy marriage, so he knows what that looks like. He should be in good health. He should be Catholic, and he should be supportive of my faith - or at least not interfere with my going to Mass. He should be capable of taking in love - of receiving love - himself. He should understand about not having sex before we're married. And we should meet through someone who knows and loves us both. Oh, and I think he should also have grown up in Illinois. That way, I'll really "get" him. But do whatever You think."

I knew it was Monday, and I knew it was Holy Week, but there was something I didn't know. Something I didn't realize until nine years later.

It was March 25. It was the Feast of the Annunciation.[1]

---

[1] The seminal moment in all human history, the moment the Angel Gabriel towered before Mary and announced God's plan to save us by coming into the world through her. Mary humbly replied, "Be it done to me according to your word."

~ What Was Broken in Me ~

A priest once told me, "People think Christianity is a religion. It's not a religion. It's a healing." In each of us, there is something broken, something God wants to heal. How we came to be broken is not as important as the fact that we are, the effect more critical than the cause. Here is what was broken in me.

My parents married in the aftermath of a personal tragedy that defined my mother's relationship with God. My mother, Val Jenkins, was the youngest of four children of Wisconsin dairy farmers. Val and her siblings had one of those Depression-poor but idyllic, rural childhoods where the children, at least, were blissfully unaware of how desperate things really were. Val entered the University of Wisconsin in Madison in 1943 and worked part-time at Wisconsin General Hospital. There she fell in love with a handsome, young intern named Jed. Jed was the well-loved son of an educated, well-to-do family in Madison, and Val felt welcomed into their world of privilege with open arms. Val and Jed became engaged when she was a mere 19 years old, but World War II was raging, and doctors were in critical demand, so Jed went to war. Some months later, Jed and several others were on a raft taking supplies down a river in Italy when they were ambushed by snipers from shore. Jed was the only one killed.

Val told me several times over the years how she found out Jed was dead. On a beautiful, crisp, golden autumn morning, Jed's mother telephoned Val at the hospital and broke the news. Val dropped the phone, dashed out of the hospital, and ran all the way to Jed's family's home. When Val was almost there, she saw Jed's mother coming out of the house, and they ran to each other and fell to the ground, sobbing in each other's arms. I don't know how long it was before Val left there, but the next thing she did was go back to her own room, frantically tear up everything she had ever written and mound it all up into a bonfire. Val was a promising young writer, but she was so angry at God for taking the love of her life that she burned it all, every journal, every poem, every manuscript. She told me, "My talent came from God, so I didn't want any part of it. I didn't want to have anything to do with God ever again."

Val and my biological father, Bob Acker, were already friends, and as she put it later, "He made me laugh, and he wanted to marry me. I had no use for my life anymore, so I thought, 'I don't care about my life, but he does, so why not marry him?'" Still shell shocked from the loss of her dead hero Jed, she numbly stumbled into marriage with Bob when she was 20.

Bob had baggage of his own. His parents, James and Lenora, had lost their first born, Elmer, when he was 16 years old, three years before Bob was even conceived. They lost their second son, Russell, at age eight when Bob was only four years old. Bob was born already broken, swaddled in survivor's guilt. I have a black and white photograph of him as a jug-eared, Catholic school boy, sad-eyed and somber, the "heir and the spare" long gone and him alone to carry on. When he finally left home, he must have felt some hope that he could leave that mantle behind, find someone who didn't keep looking through him for the one who was supposed to be there.

He chose wrong. So did she. But they had their reasons just like the rest of us. We congratulate ourselves on setting sail for a brave, new world, but our "reasons" camouflage the coming calamity. Bob was in

6

love, but maybe he loved the comfort of already knowing how to be second best. Maybe to punish his Catholic, mourning mother, he chose a Protestant so angry at God, not only wouldn't she convert, she wouldn't even step foot in the church of his childhood. Maybe Val chose a cradle Catholic to make that very point herself, to shake her fist at God. Or maybe they were drawn to each other because their brokenness locked into place at precisely the same point. The place where there was only leftover love.

It was there they had me.

They couldn't make it work, and she left him when I was three years old.

It's hard to hate a man, but love his child, to hate God, but love what God created. After my parents' divorce, my mother struggled both financially and psychologically for several years. A vivacious, athletic woman in her youth, Val was now bitter and depressed. My only memories of her are all from the side, never of her looking me in the face. She would probably tell you she wasn't aware she never looked at me, but that wasn't my experience. I was shunned.

Most of my childhood is buried beyond my memory, but I do remember a story my mother sometimes told me, always looking out the window as she spoke:

"I had to leave you with other adults during the day while I worked, so I decided I had to discipline you to do whatever an adult told you to do without hesitation. But when you were about four years old, something happened that made me see I had gone too far. You and I were leaving our apartment, and you started running down the hallway. I wanted you to quiet down and walk, so I called your name. I didn't even yell, I just said your name once in a normal voice. As soon as you heard my voice, you immediately stopped in mid-stride and stood there in exactly the same position, completely still like a

7

statue, without moving and barely breathing. That's when I knew I'd gone too far."

I don't recall that episode, but I do have a picture of myself that is very telling. There I am at age four, standing in our living room, hair held back by barrettes, curls cascading down past my shoulders, wearing a white, starched, peter pan collared blouse under a corduroy jumper, curtsying stiffly and smiling a wooden smile, not into the camera, but up and to the left, at my mother taking the picture. Ever since I can remember, whenever I see that picture, I tell myself, "That's a trained seal." That's how I was then and how I continued to be until Harry. Masquerading.

As for Bob Acker, after my mother left him, I saw him only once. I fabricated a fiction about him that I staunchly believed for most of my life. Bob was a cradle Catholic, and I mistakenly believed that if a Catholic got divorced, he or she was automatically excommunicated from the Church. I understood "excommunicated" to mean banished from God's sight. Eternally. Since my parents were divorced, I concluded that Bob, and by extension I, had been excommunicated. I was the child of one parent who had turned away and one who'd been thrown away. From every angle I could see, God had no use for me. God was angry at me. God had hurled me to another planet where He never even visited. I was an outsider everywhere.

Leaving my childhood, the pieces I packed up and took with me were the Hit Parade of fears for much of mankind. You might share one or two. First was my belief that my presence on the planet was accidental, and the ever present feeling of holding my breath, always one step from disaster. The axiom of abandonment and all its corollaries. The certainty that marriage was combustible. Most of all, I carried one conviction in my core; love was not to be believed. Someone might say they loved me, but give it time. Sooner of later, they'd get to know me, and then they'd change their mind.

God included.

In years to come, there were plenty of people I loved, and people who said they loved me, but there was also plenty of data confirming my conviction. Nothing happened to convince me otherwise.

Until Harry.

"Trained Seal"

"I'm having this fantasy that you're going to marry my dad."
- Harry's daughter, Jennifer

~ The Annunciation ~

We think prayer is us trying to talk God into something. I think it's the opposite. It's God finally talking us into His plan. It's us finally getting on board. A cosmic "Captain May I" where God doesn't take a step until we say, "Yes."

On Wednesday of Holy Week, 2002, two days after my prayer, Harry's oldest daughter, Jennifer, who worked for me at the time, came into my office, closed the door, sat down, and announced completely out of the blue,

"I know you're my boss, and I hope this doesn't scare you, but I keep having this fantasy that you're going to marry my dad. But he lives in Charlotte, and you live in Raleigh, so I don't know how you're going to get together."

She kept talking, but I had no idea what she was saying because of the alarm going off in my head. I was right. God had taken my prayer and run with it. In my head, I was shouting at God, trying to reel Him back with,

"What are you thinking?! I didn't mean now. I meant in a few years!!

This is exactly why I didn't want to bring this up with You!"

And so forth.

But in spite of my shock, I knew two things that day. I knew her father and I would marry, and I knew that it hadn't been my idea. God had been waiting for me to come around to His way of thinking. God had waited for my "yes". And I said, "Yes" on the Feast of the Annunciation.

Just as Gabriel had announced to Mary that the Lord was coming for all of us, God made an announcement loudly and clearly.

Harry was coming for me.

"My plan was to drink myself to death."
- Harry

~ What Was Broken in Harry ~

Harry, like me, was the child of an Irish Catholic father, also named Harry, and a Protestant mother, Myrtle. Unlike my parents, though, Harry's were very much in love, and Myrtle was strongly committed to her future husband and their children. So Myrtle converted to Catholicism, and the two were married on July 29, 1939 at the Old Cathedral in Alton, Illinois where Harry and his three brothers were all baptized as well. Myrtle was a gorgeous, vivacious woman, and a talented musician, but her family's hardscrabble subsistence left her with a jaded wariness of "getting taken" which she passed on to her sons. In the mid-1920s, she played piano in an all-female band called The Rhythm Queens, and later became the only female member of a ragtime band popular in the Alton area in the early 1930s. Harry's father was a chemical engineer at the Shell Oil Refinery in Wood River, Illinois, so the happy synergy of their complementary DNA produced a wonderful left/right brain balance in Harry. He once told me that when he was an engineering student at the University of Missouri, he took all the English courses he could, "...for the easy A."

Harry's parents doted on their sons. Harry's earliest memory was of a time at about age two when he was sitting companionably on the front porch steps with his father whom he adored, and they were discussing going and getting an ice cream cone.

Harry told me, "I grew up a cultural Catholic," with more focus on form than substance. Every Saturday night, Myrtle tied a dishrag around the kitchen faucet so that they would all remember not to get a drink of water after midnight in readiness for receiving the Holy Eucharist[1]. His father was a lector, standing up in front of the congregation and doing one of the readings at Mass on Sunday morning, but Harry's main memory was that the church got so hot and stuffy that people, including his father, sometimes passed out cold and had to be carried away.

However, Harry also remembered a profound moment when he was 16 years old which made a deep impression on him. At that time, he was a Boy Scout in a troop led by his father. It was early spring, the time of year when sirens sound tornado warnings every afternoon, and most Illinoisans spend the evening barricaded in the basement, waiting for the threat to lift. This particular spring had been especially bad, and tornadoes thundered through leveling everything for miles around. Harry's troop volunteered to help in the aftermath and was assigned to set up a makeshift shelter in a local Protestant church. Harry had never been in a Protestant church before, had never been in anything but a Catholic church. Here is how he remembered it:

"I walked into the sanctuary of the church and was immediately struck by how cold it was. Not temperature cold, but desolate. I couldn't figure out why until I realized there was no Eucharist there. It felt cold and empty."

It was a stark realization he never forgot.

Another important influence on Harry was that his parents sent him to school at Saint Bernard's, the small parochial school attached to

13

their church. The nuns who ran the school were a group of passionate young women who had just come north after working for civil rights in the Deep South. Sister Angela was the principal of the school, and Harry was impressed by her most of all.

Harry and I once made a Great Nostalgia Trip back to our roots in Illinois, and Harry took me to see the school. He lovingly pointed out the third floor window where Sister Angela, dressed in a tight, white wimple and woolen habit, jumped in place, flapping her arms up and down, leading her small charges on the playground below in rousing daily calisthenics. She knew each of them not only by name, but by heart. Knew each of their strengths and talents. Every Christmas, she wrote each student a little note, lifting them up, highlighting specific good points they had and encouraging them along a particular path she saw for them. Harry was touched by her kindness and care, and it was Sister Angela who started Harry thinking about becoming a Jesuit. When she made it clear to him that he could be a priest and a scientist at the same time, he decided that was what he wanted to do. It was only when he discovered girls in high school that his plans got derailed.

Harry spent most of his professional life doing cutting-edge research at Bell Laboratories in Murray Hill, New Jersey, amassing more than 40 patents. When I knew him, he only talked about that time if I asked, always downplaying his achievements. Once, though, we were watching the movie *October Sky*, the story of NASA engineer Homer Hickam. Harry had previously read Hickam's wonderful book *Rocket Boys*, and he was moved all over again by the movie. He told me as the end credits rolled, "That was me. That was my life. Small-town wunderkind makes good." He didn't elaborate on what "makes good" meant, but I later learned he had been a pioneering researcher at Bell Labs, at Max Planck Institute for Metallurgy in Stuttgart, Germany, and at Philips Research Laboratories in Eindhoven, the Netherlands. I told him once he was the smartest person I'd ever known, but he dismissed that idea, saying,

"You don't know what smart is. I was hanging around with guys who had their sights on the Nobel Prize."

Harry married a local girl he met one summer when he and his brothers had been playing tennis and stopped at an A&W stand for a root beer float. Janet was working as a carhop there and was the most beautiful girl Harry had ever seen. Like Myrtle, Janet grew up dirt poor, met her "Prince Charming" in Harry, and converted to Catholicism, so they could be married in the Catholic Church. Harry grew up watching the model of his parents' strong marriage, but there was something else he saw happen. When his grandfather died, his grandmother climbed up the stairs to their bedroom and died the next day. Harry's twin brother, Larry, once told me he thought Harry took love too seriously. I think Harry learned love was the most serious thing of all.

Harry's career took them to live in Germany and the Netherlands. They had John and Jennifer two years apart and then their last, "surprise" baby, Jill, several years later. Harry and Janet suffered through several major family crises and cataclysms, both physical and emotional, and Jennifer once described her father to me as "a broken man." The last crisis was Janet's battling breast cancer for well over a decade. Harry told me he sometimes felt guilty because he thought he pushed her to keep trying new treatments long after she was ready to give up. Although they raised their children in the Catholic Church and sent them to Catholic school, during Janet's illness, she found it difficult to go to church. She felt like all she did at Mass was cry, so they stopped going completely. Shortly before Janet died, she told Harry, "Give me a year of mourning. Then find someone to marry."

Janet died in October, 1994. Harry took her death hard. After her funeral, he talked alone with the priest for nearly two hours. Whatever comfort or wisdom the priest had to offer didn't make a dent. Harry left and never looked back. He was angry with God and turned his back on Him for good. Or so he thought.

About 6 years after Janet died, Harry began seeing a woman he met online. He told me that he never loved her or intended to marry her and even felt his relationship with her, "...dishonored my marriage to Janet." He told me, "I just wanted someone in the seat next to me pointing things out as we rode along." His family did not like this woman, however, and his daughter Jennifer confronted him saying she would only see her father when this woman was not there. That was it. Harry immediately broke off the relationship, resigning himself to a life alone. He went into a mental cave, and he told me,

"I intended to retire to the lake and end my life in a socially acceptable way. My plan was to drink myself to death."

He had no use for his life, and he had no use for God.

God thought differently.

1 Catholics believe that at Mass communion wafers and wine are miraculously transformed into the body and blood of Christ. This transformed bread and wine are called the Eucharist. At this time, Catholics did not eat or drink anything after midnight in preparation for receiving the Eucharist at Mass.

Harry at 3 years old

"You're the most depressing person I ever met."
- Harry

~ Our First Meeting ~

In the months following Jennifer's revelation in my office, time seemed to pick up speed. Jennifer started campaigning with both Harry and me to get us to meet. Harry lived in Charlotte, North Carolina and worked at the University of North Carolina there, but he made frequent trips to Raleigh, so there were ample opportunities for us to meet. However, neither Harry nor I was anxious to get this party started. I was still stunned by the sudden onset of what was apparently God's plan, and Harry was still in his mental cave. Both of us were resistant and stubbornly noncommittal.

I firmly believed, though, that this new and alarming situation was God's response to my prayer, so I did the only thing I knew to do. I prayed. A friend had told me about a 54-day rosary novena that she had prayed for help in deciding whether to marry her husband or not. Each day of the novena you pray a rosary for a particular intention. For the first 27 days, you pray in petition for the intention, and the next 27 days, you pray in thanksgiving for the answer to the petition. My friend told me that in her experience, sometime during the 54 days, an answer always came. I decided to pray that if God intended that Harry and I should marry, both of us would respond and accept His plan for us. I started the rosary novena on June 27, 2002, three months after my prayer during Holy Week.

18

Jennifer was planning to move from North Carolina to New York City in August of 2002 and go to grad school at Fordham University, so she had been stepping up the pressure on each of us to make something happen before she left. In mid-July, Harry called me for the first time. All business, he said,

"I'm getting a lot of pressure from Jennifer, and you probably are too. Let's just get her off our backs before she leaves."

Oddly relieved by his clear lack of interest, I said that sounded like a good idea.

"How about if we just have coffee or lunch or something?" he asked in a monotone.

"Either one is fine with me," I answered, equally noncommittal.

"I have to be in Raleigh next Wednesday. How about if we have lunch?" he said without enthusiasm.

I turned to Wednesday in my calendar and said that would be fine. Harry said he'd come pick me up at 11:30. We hung up, and I sank shakily into my chair. Wednesday, July 24. Why did that ring a bell? The last day of petition in my novena was July 23, 2002. The first day of thanksgiving was July 24. The first time we would meet was July 24th, the first day of thanksgiving in my novena.

On the morning of July 24, Jennifer came into my office with a dozen roses for me saying,

"At least you'll get flowers from somebody today."

Roses are usually associated with the Blessed Mother, so I was a little taken aback.

19

Harry finally got to my office about 10 minutes later, flustered and out of breath, saying,

"You know all those doors around the bottom floor of the building? I opened every one of them."

He asked if I had somewhere in mind for us to go for lunch, and I suggested a little coffee and sandwich shop in the next town over, Fuquay-Varina. As we pulled out of the parking lot in his green Toyota Highlander, I asked him,

"Do you believe in fate?"

"No," he barked without hesitation.

It was not an auspicious beginning. When we got to the cafe, we ordered tuna sandwiches and sat down and talked. We talked for the next two and a half hours. We talked about every conceivable thing. Talking with him felt like breathing pure oxygen. I felt so clearheaded, so completely conscious and present. And a little lightheaded. I'd never experienced anything like this before in my life. My impression was that he was like all my midwestern male relatives rolled into one. I knew him. When Harry told me he had grown up in Alton, Illinois, I wanted to look up to Heaven and say,

"Now You're just showing off."

Even though we were conversing, I could see that Harry was guarded and closed off. True to his word, he seemed clearly to just be interested in getting Jennifer off his back, and he didn't show any sign of interest in me. Quite the contrary. At one point, I told him the heartfelt story of a friend who had adopted several siblings from a Russian orphanage. Harry leaned back in his chair, firmly folded his arms, and frowned,

"You're the most depressing person I ever met."

Outwardly, I just smiled. Inwardly, I thought, "You won't always think that."

When Harry drove me back to work, he said it was nice meeting me, but didn't make any allusion to the future. I was not surprised. Nonetheless, when I got back to my office, I told a friend I thought we were going to get married if he ever came out of his cave. She looked at me worriedly and gently suggested maybe it would be nice to just have Harry as a friend. I understood what she was driving at, but I knew she was wrong. I told my sisters the same thing, and they had the same worried reaction. All my friends and family worried I was constructing an increasingly vivid fantasy.

Journal entry–July 25, 2002

My friends are afraid I'll put too much stock in meeting Harry – that I'll talk myself into believing he and I were put together by God–that I'll misunderstand God's purpose. Phaedra, though, on Tuesday, on hearing it was the last day of the petition phase of the 54 day novena, said, "Oh, you two are so getting married."

I think what I'm supposed to believe in is the immensity of God's love. It's not an issue of pretending or believing in romantic love or human love. It's the certainty of trusting in God's love and His loving Providence. "The moment one definitely commits oneself, then Providence moves too." I don't think God would go to such lengths to put us together just as e-mail pals. (And as I am writing this in the Perpetual Adoration Chapel, I can smell roses. I asked the young woman behind me if she could smell them, and she smiled and said no.)

I will keep counsel only with God. He is the one I spoke to about this. He is

21

the one who answered. Everything else is speculation. God doesn't speculate.
He answers. And He has (roses again). Thank you, Father, my sweet Father.

Harry had given me no indication that he ever wanted to see me again, and had I not prayed my prayer, I would have thought that was the end of it. But I *had* prayed, and God had presented me with a man who fit my list exactly. And we had met on the first day of the start of my rosary novena prayers of thanksgiving.

I had no confidence in Harry.

I had complete confidence in God.

"I think I'm supposed to join the Catholic Church."
- Eileen

~ Lassoed ~

The Blessed Mother Mary will hike up her skirts and wade into what-ever mess you've gotten yourself into to bring you to her son.

My spiritual history was spotty. I spent much of my early childhood with my mother's parents in Clintonville, Wisconsin. At my grand-parents' house, on the wall of the small bedroom where I slept hung a pair of pictures of towheaded toddlers praying in profile, one a small boy, the other a girl. Maybe you remember those pictures from your childhood, too. I studied them before I went to sleep and remember them vividly. Gram taught me a common child's prayer that I said every night,

> *Now I lay me down to sleep*
> *I pray the Lord my soul to keep,*
> *If I should die before I wake*
> *I pray the Lord my soul to take.*

That prayer and what I was praying for were a mystery to me. It had everything to do with how precarious life was and nothing to do with who God was, and I always felt a little forlorn after praying.

Every Sunday, Gram and I walked down to Christ Congregational Church. Gram had attended the Methodist church for awhile, but concluded the Methodists were "too high-society," and so, for no more theological reason than that, we were Congregationalists. The church was an imposing red brick building, in my memory dark and dank inside, but the music was moving and mournful. "Rock of Ages," "Nearer My God to Thee," "The Old Rugged Cross." Hearing those songs today takes me right back to the pew sitting with Gram. The seed Gram planted in me was the thought that someone was out there. Who that was, I had no idea.

Before Bob Acker was gone from my life, he gave me one experience that proved providential. When I was five, Bob and his new wife, Lois, took me to visit his parents in Fort Atkinson, Wisconsin, and there we all went to a Mass at Saint Joseph's Catholic Church. Unlike the darkness of the Congregational Church in Clintonville, Saint Joseph's seemed to me bright and airy, packed with parishioners. The altar rested on two statues of kneeling, golden angels. There was the sweet smell of incense and the lovely chiming of bells. There was life there. I could feel it, even at that young age, and I thought, "These people know something."

My first personal experience of God was when I was eight years old. Clintonville was a very small town, and I was allowed free rein to wander wherever I wanted. One day, I'd been walking and walking, not paying any attention to where I was going, when I suddenly realized I had no idea where I was. None. Turning round and round, I started to panic. My head started pounding, and my throat started tightening. Nothing looked familiar. No direction held any clue. As I turned once more, for some reason I decided to look up to the sky. Then I saw it. The steeple of a church in the distance towering high above the houses. I knew that church. I knew where it was. I knew I just had to keep my eyes up and keep walking toward that steeple, and I could find my way. At that moment, I understood that, without

24

my asking, God had reached down and helped me. It was years before I learned I could ask, and He'd help every time.

Back home in Milwaukee, nine years old, I sequestered myself in my room secretly keeping a scrap book of articles about the popes. Pictures from *Life* magazine, articles from the *Milwaukee Journal...* . Pope Pius XII, John XXIII. Powerful stuff, but I still believed I was relegated to always be exiled. Eternally not good enough. Years later, I learned that in fact my parents had *not* been married in the Catholic Church or any church. Only recently, I also learned that Bob's mother, Lenora, was a first generation, Irish Catholic who was distressed by her only living son marrying outside the Church and not having her first and only grandchild baptized in the Church. Though I never saw her after the age of five, I have no doubt Lenora continued praying for me. Her prayers brought her son back to the Church, and decades later, her prayers brought me to the Church as well.

Two grandmothers, one who pointed me toward God, and one who put me on the path.

After my marriage to my daughters' father ended, I was badly in need of hope with nowhere to find it. A friend from work told me she had gotten a lot of encouragement and direction from a psychic, and that she trusted what the psychic had to say. I called the psychic, and she gave me a reading right over the phone. Over time, I became more and more dependent on these readings, on anything she could predict. After these sessions, I was often astounded but never calmed. Mainly, I felt more and more urgently that I had to hear what she had to say. After awhile, we talked almost every day. If I could have had her talk to me every waking moment, I would have.

In March, 1995, my psychic and I went to Myrtle Beach, South Carolina for a weekend. I was still under her spell, but I also had with me *The Way of Perfection* by Saint Teresa of Avila. I don't remember why

I'd started reading that or how I came by a copy, but I'd started it and thought enough of it to bring it with me that weekend. The day we got to Myrtle Beach, we went to a new-age rock shop with bins of geodes, crystals, etc. I walked down the aisles of new-age paraphernalia and suddenly came upon something completely out of context. A 10 inch, ebony statue of a woman standing on a sphere, clothed in a long robe and veil, praying hands pointing upward, with what seemed to be a large halo over her head. Very modern, clean lines. I was transfixed. Something drew me powerfully to that statue, and it was the only one there. I picked it up and held it while I walked around some more, but I'd lost interest in anything but that statue. When we got back to the hotel, my psychic friend and I talked about the statue. She turned it over and over in her hands telling me she was "getting" something. She said I was drawn to the statue because I'd been a nun in another life, and then, suddenly "inspired", claimed I'd actually been Saint Teresa of Avila in another life. That's how evil works. It puffs up your pride. I didn't believe her, but I did wonder why I was so powerfully drawn to the statue.

That night when I went to bed, I put the statue on the nightstand next to me and stared at it in the moonlight coming through the window. I sensed that the statue was something important, and I understood that it meant something. I just couldn't understand the halo.

The year after the Myrtle Beach trip, this same psychic and I set out on a whirlwind road trip from Raleigh to Taos, New Mexico. She wanted to go because that area of the country is so heavily new-age. I wanted to go to stay in the desert at Ghost Ranch where Georgia O'Keeffe had lived and painted. So we set out together with no idea what a life changing trip we were embarking on. When we got to Taos, we checked into a hotel and then went to the town center. There we found a tarot-card reader, and we both had "readings" done. I really didn't pay that much attention to what she was saying. It all sounded pretty generic. She did, however, say two things that proved prophetic. The first was the directive, "Go where your feet lead you." Obvious, huh? The second was, "You're going to get a gift from God." That got my attention.

After our readings, my friend wanted to go back to the hotel to take a nap, so I told her I still wanted to buy a bear fetish necklace and was going to walk the short distance back to the town center to look for one. As I walked along toward town, across the road, I saw a small, dingy, dirty looking, indoor flea market. I paid no attention and walked on, but I suddenly felt provoked to go over there. I ignored the feeling and continued walking, but I again felt compelled to go across the street into the flea market. Again, I ignored it thinking, "I really, really want a bear fetish necklace." The same feeling overcame me a third time. At that point, I was a little confused since I absolutely did not want to go to this obviously unseemly market and was intent on getting that necklace. But I remembered what the tarot-reader had said, so I decided to "go where my feet led me." Perplexed, I walked across the street.

It was 5:45 p.m., and the flea market closed at 6:00. Inside, there were two long rows of dusty glass display counters. I started up one side thinking, "There must be a really cool bear fetish necklace inside here somewhere." I scrutinized each display looking for the necklace I assumed I was going to find. Nothing. I continued along, still seeing nothing of any interest, until I turned the corner and started down the row of counters on the other side. At the first counter, I stopped stock-still. There was a large, black, wooden rosary artfully hung inside the display case. It knocked the breath out of me. I stood transfixed. I couldn't speak. The gentleman behind the counter finally asked,

"Is there something I can show you?"

"How much is that rosary?" I finally managed, still staring at the rosary.

27

"Four dollars."

He explained that he often drove up into the hills and bought items from religious who were selling what few personal belongings they had to support their small communities. The rosary once belonged to a nun who had worn it around her waist. He took it out, and I held it in my hands, slowly working the silver crucifix between my fingers. We talked and talked, and he told me about a place in the hills he said I should visit. El Santuario de Chimayo. He told me about the pilgrimages thousands of people made there each Easter and that many people believed healings took place there. His own daughter had gone there and been healed of uterine cancer. After nearly an hour, I finally said I had to go, and asked him again how much the rosary was. He looked at me for a moment, reached out and closed my hand around the rosary, and answered,

"It's a gift."

His words brought me up short. I put the rosary around my neck and walked out in a trance. I felt so at peace, so lifted. More at peace than I had in years as if I could finally breathe. Get a good lung full of clean air. I was to have that same feeling again every time I talked to Harry.

During the rest of the trip, I had an overwhelming feeling of being led and protected. As my psychic and I set out on our way back home, we talked about what we each had learned on the trip. She told me of her own, I thought frightening and dangerous, adventures in the desert with some other new-agers. She believed something extraordinary had happened in the desert, and she said she felt she had been transfused with "more power" than ever before. She asked what I had concluded about my own experiences, and all I could say was,

"I think I'm supposed to join the Catholic Church."

My friend denigrated the idea as archaic and reactionary, but the power her opinion had over me was gone. I was rock solid in my conviction.

The Blessed Mother had lassoed me with a rosary.

I knew what I was supposed to do.

"God is still indulging me."
- Eileen

~ I Fall in Love ~

In October, 1998, I started unaccountably thinking about petitioning to have my marriage annulled. Why this idea kept coming into my head, I had no idea. It made no sense to me. If your marriage had ended in divorce, you could not marry again in the Church unless the first marriage was annulled (declared not to have been a valid marriage according to Canon Law), but I had no intention of ever marrying again, so I couldn't see why an annulment mattered to me. More importantly, it certainly did not seem to be my idea at all. Still, the idea persisted until it became almost a compulsion. I told a friend about this who wisely counseled, "There's some reason the Holy Spirit is pushing you so hard about this. You better not ignore it." So I applied for an annulment and found the year-long process both humbling and healing. At the end, I was granted an annulment and thought my spiritual growth and healing was the reason. That was only one of the reasons.

In the fall of 2001, long before my prayer and my first meeting with Harry, I decided to sell the house my former husband and I had shared and move my daughter, Phaedra, and myself into a different house. I needed the equity, but more importantly, I needed a new start. There were too many flashbacks, too many ghosts at every turn in that house. Besides, Phaedra would be heading off to college in just a little over a year. I wanted to have a little time for the two of us to make some good memories in a new house, some time for a new place to feel like home for both of us before she left. So I set about making repairs and getting the old house ready to sell. I had no idea how liberating the process would be.

One day, I was having lunch with an acquaintance at work. We barely knew each other and had only spoken over the phone a couple times, but we started chatting, and I told her about getting my house ready to sell. She listened, smiling, and finally asked,

"Are you dating anyone?"

"What? No. What does that have to do with selling my house?"

"It has everything to do with it."

With that she launched into the saga of how she met her husband. She had been in a situation similar to mine. She had been married, but it ended badly, and she concluded she never wanted to marry again. She sold the house she and her husband had shared and bought a small brick house that she loved. She was very happy to be settling into a place of her own when WHAM! She met a man, had a whirlwind romance, and they married shortly thereafter.

"I didn't even have all the boxes unpacked before we got married!" she glowed.

I saw where this was going, and I didn't want to go there.

"Interesting," I said politely, though I was anything *but* interested.

"Yes! This is going to happen to you, too. I predict you'll no sooner

31

get moved into your new house before you meet a man and get married," she said with a nod.

I hadn't even prayed my prayer yet, and I was decidedly uninterested in getting married, but I was nonetheless nonplussed. I knew these kinds of conversations didn't happen for no reason, but I'm good at ignoring what I don't want to see.

After our first meeting in July 2002, all was quiet on the Harry front. Jennifer kept taking each of our emotional pulses, but Harry's didn't seem to register. I began to think I'd gotten it all wrong. Every week or so, I sent Harry a short, chatty e-mail just to keep the door open, and though he always answered, he never initiated.

At that point in my life, I still thought God was angry at me, and I started to wonder whether He was making some kind of point about my unworthiness. In August, I was at In His Name Catholic bookstore in Raleigh, and I ran into Marguerite (daughter of the owners Tom and Marguerite Sr.), the manager. Marguerite asked me how things were going, and for some reason, I poured out the whole story to her: my prayer, Jennifer's response, my rosary novena, our first meeting falling on the first day of thanksgiving of the novena, Jennifer's giving me roses the morning of our meeting, and Harry's fulfilling everything on my list including having grown up in Illinois. Then I told her how nothing further had happened, and maybe I'd fabricated the whole situation. Maybe I was supposed to remain by myself after all. Marguerite patiently listened to the whole saga, and then she surprised me by saying,

"How many signs are you looking for? How many signs will convince you? You need to work on recognizing signal graces. God wants you to be happy. You deserve it."

What?! Had I been looking at everything the wrong way?

As I walked out of the store pondering her response, I ran into another friend, Al Benthall, who had overheard me telling Marguerite the story. At that time, Al had been praying and trying to decide whether God was calling him to be a priest. Al was well familiar with the process of trying to discern God's will. Although we were pondering two different kinds of situations, Al and I were dealing with the same issue. Each of us was struggling with the problem of wanting ever more signs before we'd believe the ones we'd already been given. Al is very devout and a very clear thinker, and I was completely overwhelmed to hear him tell me,

"God works on getting us to detach from the world and then slowly introduces the things He wants us to be attached to back into our lives. We're not meant to be hermits. The fact that the roses and the lunch were on the first day of the thanksgiving part of the novena is significant - it's a sign of God's love."

I went back home that day feeling fortified.

By the fall of 2002, however, Harry still seemed very much in his cave, and I began again to doubt. I didn't doubt that God had put us together, but I doubted that I understood His intent. Maybe I was in purgatory on Earth. Maybe God was mad at me and rubbing my nose in my past mistakes. One afternoon when I went to pick up Phaedra at school, I ran into a priest, Father Dougherty, in the school library. On the spur of the moment, I asked him,

"Father, do you think that God sometimes shows you how wonderful life could have been if you hadn't screwed up so badly?"

Father Dougherty looked at me for a long moment with an expression that said, "Where did we go wrong with you?" and said,

"No, but someone else certainly does. That's not how God works. Do

33

you want to tell me what's going on?"

So I once again repeated the entire story to him, leaving nothing out. Father Dougherty listened without interruption. When I was finished, he said,

"Let me be sure I've got this right. You prayed and asked God for a very specific present. Then God came back with exactly what you asked for all wrapped up with a big bow tied around it. All you have to do is untie the bow and open the present. I'm sorry, what's your question again?"

Father just smiled and waited for this to sink in. I slowly smiled back, and he continued,

"The phone lines go from here to Charlotte, too, you know. You can always call him yourself."

"Father, I could never do that!" I gasped.

Could I?

In February 2003, I learned that a well known priest was going to be speaking in Charlotte at Saint Gabriel's Catholic Church. I wanted to hear this priest, but I also thought this seemed like a suspiciously tailor-made excuse to see Harry. It had the feel of a golden opportunity that I shouldn't let pass me by. So in early February, I e-mailed in as nonchalant a tone as I could muster,

Hello Harry,

This coming Saturday, I will be in Charlotte for most of the day (9:30 to about 4) at St. Gabriel Catholic Church. I don't know how close that is to

you, but I was hoping you might have time to come have a cup of coffee with me before I head back to Raleigh.

Take care,
Eileen

To my delight, Harry wrote back,

As it currently stands, I should be on Lake Wiley from 7 a.m. until 2 p.m. fishing with my club. This may well change as the weather report is not promising. Stay tuned. If I can do so, I would be happy to get together with you for coffee (the Lutheran drink...a little Lake Wobegon humor here).

Best,
H

He would be happy to get together? This sounded promising, and I replied,

Hope to see you - I'll wear my waders.

Eileen

The next day, Harry wrote,

Saturday is to be a day of cold rain. My fishing club normally ignores such stuff, and we may well fish. I won't know until tomorrow sometime. If we don't fish, I will be happy. I no longer have the need to prove my manhood by being miserable for 8 hours of fishing in the cold rain. On the other hand, if the club fishes, I will go. (It's a man thing.) I hope to know the answer soon, i.e., tomorrow afternoon. I'll let you know as soon as I know.

Jen told me that she will be in NC in March. I intend to travel to the dreaded

Triangle to see her then. I hope that the three of us can have lunch or some-
thing then.

Now we were getting somewhere. Whatever happened, Harry was looking past the coming weekend and talking about getting together further down the road.

As it happened, the weather worked in our favor. The forecast changed to a prediction of snow, and Harry did not go fishing. He was supposed to meet me outside Saint Gabriel's at 4:00 p.m. Inside the church, the priest was talking about how it was okay to be angry with God, how God could take it, and how you could go ahead and tell Him how angry you were. This described Harry perfectly. It was bitterly cold out, and so I was hoping and praying he would come in at least to the vestibule, so he would hear the priest talking about anger. But when the session was over, and I turned around to look, Harry wasn't there. He was outside standing on the sidewalk, looking up at the snowy sky.

We went to Starbucks and had a latte, and Harry regaled me with stories about the doings of the real-life Johnny Appleseed from a book he'd just finished reading. I didn't love him yet, but I again had that heady feeling that being with him was like breathing pure oxygen. But Harry was concerned about me driving back to Raleigh in the coming snow storm, so after about an hour, he convinced me I needed to get on the road. He also said he would come to Raleigh when Jennifer was there in March. I was very low. I misread his concern and thought he wasn't interested in spending anymore time with me. I drove back to Raleigh in a funk. I couldn't see he was any closer to coming out of the cave.

However, that little encounter was enough to start me e-mailing Harry more regularly, and I wrote to him in a way I'd never communicated with any other man. I just wrote straightforwardly about anything that was in my head without worrying about how he would react. One night, unable to sleep for thinking about him, I got up in the middle of the night and wrote him,

Tonight I'm thinking about you. Do you know the book, On the Spine of Time: An Angler's Love of the Smokies *by Harry Middleton? A mountain-born friend of mine has a 17 year old son who has been fly fishing with a passion since he was 7 years old, and she recommended it to me saying that the luscious language alone made it worth reading. So I've been reading along, stupefied by the vibrance of his descriptions, and now I wish I could talk with you about nearly every paragraph. Listen: "I came to those worn-out hills as something of a refugee, a boy looking for more than just escape or insularity. Instead, I found myself in what seemed like the very eye of life's burning chaos. The mountains absorbed me, and I absorbed them and lived fully in their geography of light and shadow, stone and root, and cascading streams full of mercurial trout. In mountains, I first discovered the feel and significance of place, a solitude so rich that at times I felt sure I could feel the earth's pulse, the mountains' measured breathing." It reminds me of that wonderful Yeats poem, "The Lake Isle of Innisfree." Do you know the one I mean?*

I will arise and go now, and go to Innisfree,
And a small cabin build there of clay and wattles made;
Nine bean rows will I have there, a hive for the honeybee,
And live alone in the bee-loud glade.

And I shall have some peace there, for peace comes dropping slow
Dropping from the veils of the morning to where the cricket sings;
There midnight's all a glimmer, and noon a purple glow,
And evening full of the linnet's wings.
I will arise and go now, for always night and day
I hear lake water lapping with low sounds by the shore;
While I stand on the roadway, or on the pavement's grey,
I hear it in the deep heart's core.

Every time I stop and read a bit, I feel like saying, "Listen to this!" and typing entire pages to you. Mainly I'm wondering whether the way he describes his thoughts and feelings is also the way you think and feel when you're standing in a river. If you haven't already read this, I'll lend you my copy when you come.

It will be good to see you.
E

The next day, Harry answered:

Wow!

I know nothing of the stuff about which you write, but would like to. The description comes close to the feeling that I have about fishing. Among my friends are professional outdoor writers who have never come close (I think) to prose of this sort. Most of them are too manly to even think in these terms. Mostly it's, here is how I caught the fish, on what, and how, technically. Of course, this does no justice to the reality of the thing at all. For a real look at the man side of the sport, see Gierach, John. Any book of his (and there are many) will give you the feeling for the thing as seen from a masculine perspective. Of course, before him was Zane Grey, who wrote not only about the West, but also about fishing. His book, Lord of Lackawaxen Creek, is a classic. Jen grew up in a family (mine) that owned a cabin in the neighborhood of the Lackawaxen River in PA, and I recall it, both the cabin and the river, with inordinate fondness. I will talk to Jen soon about her impending visit to NC.

By the time we met in March in Raleigh, I had sold my house and made an offer on another house. I was anxious to see Harry and to get his opinion on my housing adventure.

Harry arrived on a lovely Saturday afternoon. Jennifer had arrived the night before, and she, Phaedra, and I were at the kitchen table when the doorbell rang. We all three went to the foyer, and I answered the door. Harry said hello, but then did something I've never seen another person do in my life. He walked past me to Jennifer, put his arms around her and said,

"My precious child."

That is the moment I began to fall in love.

It was as if God were shining a big light down on him. I had never seen a man act so tenderly, and I was completely bowled over by how open he was, how willing he was to show how much he loved his daughter in front of Phaedra and me. I stood slack jawed until Harry finally let go of Jennifer, took Phaedra's hand, and said,

"You must be Phaedra."

Now he was greeting my own daughter with genuine warmth.

I was head over heels.

The four of us went to a Japanese restaurant, and Harry told a funny story about having dinner once on a business trip to Japan. He said they were each brought a bowl of what looked like noodles, but there was a little silver dot on the end of each strand. When he looked closer, he saw the dots were eyes. I was completely enchanted.

After dinner, we drove past the house I was in the process of buying, and Harry assured me,

"Looks like a good choice."

Finally, it was time for him to drive back to Charlotte. Jennifer tried to get him to stay the night, but he insisted on going back.

That Monday, I wrote him,

Well, you won't believe it. The house I showed you has water in the crawlspace. Last night, the seller came back with a very crabby response to my repair request, and it looked as if I were going to get stuck with a house on top of a lake (not on, not next to, but on top of). But this morning I talked with my lawyer (I will NEVER - well, probably never - again make jokes about lawyers), and he assured me that I could just walk away from this deal right this minute and make another offer on another house. SO! Today I've made an offer on a house Phaedra and I absolutely love. It's a stone's throw from the other house, so it's still within walking distance to coffee and books. The layout and flow are just wonderful - really feels like us - and the rooms are a wonderful size for our various needs - including the bedroom Phaedra and I refer to as "Jen's room." The music room in the front of the house can be cut off from the bedrooms in the back, so Phaedra can play the banjo all night without my hearing it. I can't wait for you to see it once we're all settled. And it's a few thousand less than the other house - more left for cellos and dobros and trips down the Mississippi.

I'm babbling. God's still indulging me.

Four days later, Harry responded in his typically laconic manner.

An exciting and, I think, fortunate turn of events! I hope that you get the number two house.

Undeterred, I e-mailed him a couple days later.

I've been meaning to call you, but what with inspections and packing, I haven't had the chance at a reasonable hour. I'm so happy about all this that I can't stop babbling, and I wanted to babble to you in person. I did get the second house, and we're still closing on the same date - May 29. Although I liked the first house, I was thinking of it more in terms of how fortress-like it was and how I felt like I could better protect Phaedra through the coming hurricanes, ice storms, terrorist attacks, etc. in that house. The second house is completely different - we're absolutely in love with the place. This morning as I was driving in, I was contemplating where to put the Christmas tree or whether we might even need two trees. Much different.

Here's the big thing, though - and I really wish I were sitting across from you over a cup of coffee right now sharing this with you. There is much more going on here than just moving out of one house into another. I'm filled with an amazing sense of well-being which I have not felt for probably 20 years or so and never thought I would feel again. Part of that is the relief of moving out of a house with too many ghosts. Phaedra feels that very keenly as well, and her relief, in turn, makes me feel I've done something very good for her well being. Most of this feeling, though, is that the way this has all played out has made me feel very taken care of - almost spoiled. I said before that God was indulging me, and that is precisely how it feels. The last few years, I've been determinedly optimistic through a sheer act of will - hoping against hope. Now it's like something has let loose of me - or I've let loose of it - and life has taken on a very ethereal quality. Almost weightless. Unfettered.

There was a popular song in the 70s titled "The Future's So Bright (I Gotta Wear Shades)." That's how I feel.

God was helping me let go. It was like I was wobbling along on a two-wheeler with God running along behind me holding the back of the seat.

God was grooming me for what was coming next.

41

"I said to myself, 'Wow. She's a woman.'"
-Harry

~ The Jig is Up ~

After Harry's visit to Raleigh in March 2003, Jennifer escalated her efforts with each of us, campaigning daily to get her father to call me again and then giving me increasingly panicky reports about his reticence. Harry was beginning to show signs of strain. At one point, running out of excuses, Harry said to her exasperatedly,

"What if she makes me eat tofu?!"

He was backed into a corner and hurling out everything he could lay his hands on in defense. I told Jennifer I thought she should leave him alone and let things take their course, but she was too deep in the thick of things. At one point, Harry's friends arranged a date for him with a woman named Sylvia at the university, and Harry went out with her several more times. Jennifer was worried this interloper was making inroads, so she called me one day with what she considered bad news.

"I don't want to alarm you, but my dad is dating a woman named Sylvia in Charlotte. I don't know how serious this is, but he's been out with her a few times."

Jennifer was hoping this news would propel me into action, but I still had confidence that Harry was God's answer to my prayer and that things were moving along as they should.

"Don't worry. Nothing's going to happen. Sylvia is the wrong one. She's not me."

I said it with complete confidence, and I really meant it. This wasn't my belief in Harry's intentions. It was my faith in God's intentions. I felt completely at peace.

In early June, Harry planned to go to California where he and his brothers were having a reunion at the home of his youngest brother, Don. Jennifer enlisted her Aunt Donna (wife of Harry's twin brother Larry) to talk to Harry during the reunion and try to wheedle out of him what was going on in his head about me. All through the weekend, Donna gave it a game try, but reported back that Harry was decidedly and determinedly mum.

Jennifer needn't have worried. Once when she was talking to Harry about his beliefs about God, he told her,

"If God doesn't want something to happen, there's nothing you can do to make it happen. If He does want something to happen, there's nothing you can do to stop it."

Too true. Here's what happened next.

Hello Harry,

I hope you're having a grand time this summer fishing some of those rivers and lakes you've been longing to get to and that your reunion in California gave you a chance to reconnect with family you've been missing.

I don't know whether Jen told you that she invited Phaedra and me to come to your lake house in South Carolina sometime while she and your son and daughter-in-law are there in July. I have put off answering her because I wanted to talk with you just between us about it first. I decided to e-mail you rather than call so that you wouldn't be caught off guard and be thinking one thing but feeling obligated to say another. It looks to me like this is a visit that you have all been looking forward to for awhile as a chance to relax, be yourselves, and be alone together for a few days. My oldest daughter, Jessamin, lives in Phoenix, and I know how hard it can be to arrange those times together once your kids are grown and flung thither and yon. Honestly, if I were you, I'd rather just be alone with my kids during that time, and if I were your son, I'd rather be alone with my dad and sister. While I would love to see you, I do not want to intrude on you, your family, or your time together - nor to put Phaedra and myself in any kind of awkward situation. So I wanted to give you a chance to weigh in candidly on this visit knowing that, as far as I'm concerned, you are under absolutely no obligation one way or another. I have no intention of sharing with Jen that I asked you about this, and I have a very plausible - and true - excuse for why we couldn't come - we just got two 7 week-old beagle puppies who need a lot of attention right now. Regardless of how you feel about this visit, I think the world of you.

Take care,
E

Harry answered that very night.

Thanks for the very thoughtful e-mail.

You phrased the analysis perhaps better than I could myself, you are right, and I am grateful. Please do come another time when it would be just Jen, you, Phaedra and me.

Again, thanks.
Harry

Did I detect a thaw? I answered the next day.

I just spoke with Jen and deftly (I thought) presented the puppy defense. She had me stumped for a second when she said she could call you and ask whether it would be alright to bring the puppies along. I rallied, however, and said even if it were alright with you, I still wouldn't feel comfortable given what bad bathroom citizens these two still are. I promised her, however, that we could come another time. So if Jen does ask you about my bringing the puppies, feel free to be magnanimous knowing I will hold the line at this end.

Is it just me, or is this kind of fun?

Harry replied with what was beginning to look like earnestness.

Thanks for the e-mail and for your graceful handling of this situation. Please believe that you and Phaedra are most welcome to visit with us at the lake. Maybe something could be arranged when next Jen comes to NC to meet her students. This will happen in the fall, right?

Without any pushing or prodding, Harry was very naturally taking the lead in arranging for us to see each other again. Taking a step toward the entrance to the cave. Several weeks later, Harry did invite Phaedra and me to come to the lake house in August.

The stage was set.

I am sitting in my office looking at my new cello. Although I am flabbergasted daily by the malevolent political chicanery going on here, I know that none of it would surprise you. So I won't go into detail. Suffice to say that my closest friend here - the foreign language department head - has finally had enough, and today is her last day. We have advised, consoled, entertained, and bolstered each other since I've been in this job, and this is going to be a much different place without her. I've been shilly-shallying around for 5 years about getting a cello, but two weeks ago, when she told me she had

45

another job, I snapped and ordered one right off the internet the moment she left my office. We had it sent to her parents' house in Virginia to avoid the substantial NC taxes, and so my friend went up this weekend to get it and brought it in this morning to surprise me. Do you or have you played a musical instrument? To me, it's very relaxing to practice an instrument. It requires your complete attention. Maybe working on your antique fishing rods provides the same sort of thing for you. So I'm sitting here looking at my cello and thinking about how much I'm looking forward to my first cello lesson and to spending some time relaxing at a beautiful lake in the company of wonderful people.

E

Harry answered that evening.

Thanks for the e-mail.

Nope, the music gene is missing in me. My mother was a great piano player, and my youngest brother is as well. Likewise, my son is a musician. Mendel at work. All of us did take piano lessons as kids, all but one hated it, and Mother was distraught until son #4 finally redeemed her heritage.

Congrats on the cello! If you have wanted something for 5 years, something as attainable as a cello, and don't have it, something is askew somewhere. Glad you got straightened out. As for me, the mind consuming distraction has been tennis and handball. You just can't do these things and think about other things. Now I can no longer play these games, so working with my hands on other stuff, fly rods included, is a good substitute.

I am pleased that you will make it to the lake. It is a long drive, but every time I make the trip, for me only three hours, I redetermine that it is worth it.

See you there.
H

Jennifer, Phaedra, and I arrived at Harry's South Carolina lake house on Thursday, August 14, 2003. As a thank-you gift, I had gone to Outdoor Provision Company and hand picked 20 fishing flies and a red, floatable fly box. Harry later told me,

"When I saw those flies and saw what a thoughtful and expensive gift that was, I knew the jig was up."

The next day was the Feast of the Assumption[1], and I rose early and went to Mass at a small, beautiful chapel on the Clemson University campus. The priest spoke about how sex between a husband and wife was a gift from God. How it was part of the Divine Plan. When I returned to the lake house, Harry was still the only one up. He asked me if I'd like some breakfast, and when I said yes, he set about making scrambled eggs. He was still a little disheveled in a morning way which, for me, made him look almost unbearably appealing. I sat at the kitchen counter while he slowly stirred the eggs in the pan. Still scrutinizing the eggs, he asked how Mass was. I told him it was very uplifting and that the priest talked about sex. At that, he looked up and asked,

"Did he say it was a good thing?"

"He said sex is holy and sublime," I nodded with just the hint of a smile.

Harry looked at me, twinkly eyed, for just a beat, then smiled back down at the eggs.

Later that afternoon, Phaedra was out in the kayak, Jennifer was napping, and Harry was off on an errand, so I went down to lie on the dock and read a book. I wasn't down there long at all before I fell asleep. I don't know how long I was sleeping, but I was awakened when Harry came down and joined me. I was dressed in jeans with the cuffs rolled up and a nondescript tee shirt, nothing in any way alluring, but Harry later told me,

"When I saw you lying on the dock was the first time I said to myself, 'Wow! She's a woman!'"

At the time, though, Harry kept those cards close to his chest. After awhile, we all went out for a boat ride to a lovely waterfall where Jennifer and Phaedra swam while Harry and I made small talk in the boat.

The next afternoon, our daughters were outside swimming in the cove next to the lake house. Harry and I were sitting on opposite sides of the living room. Harry looked for all the world as though he were completely engrossed in whatever he was doing on his Palm Pilot. I looked similarly fascinated by my book, but I was actually trying to think of how to strike up a conversation when suddenly Harry offered,

"Would you like to see how this works?" smiling across the room at me.

Thank heavens Harry's engineering instincts had kicked in, and he made the first move with a typically engineerish topic to hide behind - how something works. I moved across the room, sitting on the floor at the foot of his chair coyly looking up at him in what I hoped was a beguiling way. As he explained the Palm Pilot's many intriguing intricacies, we both knew what was happening, but we were keenly aware that our daughters might walk in at any moment. Sure enough, not too long after, Phaedra and Jennifer came up from the lake, chatting and laughing, wondering about dinner.

Nothing happened, but everything changed.

The next day was Sunday, and it was time for Phaedra, Jennifer and me to drive back to Raleigh. All morning, I thought about how to give Harry some kind of sign, how to up the ante just a bit given how reticent we both were. I finally decided what I was going to do. The time came to leave, and Harry walked out with us. I was so nervous, my hands were shaking. Phaedra said good-bye, and then Jennifer gave her father a long hug and said good-bye. Now was the time. Much to everyone's surprise, I went up to Harry, put my arm around his neck, kissed him on the cheek, and said,

"Thank you for a lovely visit."

I stood just a moment longer, arm still around Harry's neck, smiling into his eyes. Slowly, his face took on a look I'd never seen before. He was looking right into my eyes, smiling a completely unguarded smile. I thought that look was unmistakeable. God was giving me what I needed to have the courage to take the next step.

Harry watched me get into the car and stood waving as we pulled out. We had barely gotten down the road when Jennifer said,

"I've only seen my dad look like that one other time - when he looked at my mother."

[1] Catholic tradition holds that after the completion of her earthly life, Mary was assumed body and soul into Heaven. The Feast of the Assumption commemorates Mary's assumption.

"It's time to cowboy up."
- Eileen

~ Harry Comes Out of the Cave ~

Holy Spirit, Heart Whisperer. So gentle you think each thought is your own idea. Maybe not.

For the next couple of weeks after coming back from Harry's lake house, a feeling started gaining strength inside me. It was becoming almost intolerable not knowing what Harry was thinking and feeling about us, or if he even thought in terms of "us." I decided it was time to do something. I was overwhelmed by the feeling that we needed to move past the apparent logjam where we were stuck and that it was worth taking a chance to learn what was in Harry's heart. This was a complete departure from my previous patience in waiting for him to come out of his cave, but something had to change. Looking back, I know now the Holy Spirit was working hard to get me to take a step forward. Step out in faith.

First, I called my levelheaded sister, Christie and asked what she thought of my writing to Harry and telling him how I felt. I could hear by her tone that my very wise and diplomatic sister was trying to figure out how to gently tell me she thought that I was delusional. So I called my marshmallow-hearted sister, Laura, and put the same question to her. Laura, too, struggled with how to gently dissuade me

50

from certain disaster. They were both still worried that this was all in my head and wanted to spare me from making a fool of myself.

But the feeling inside me continued to crescendo until I was almost powerless to resist. Still needing someone - anyone - to tell me to take the leap of faith, I called my brother-in-law, Bill, to see if I could get a different answer from a man's point of view. I told him my whole story and the salient points of the e-mail I was drafting in my head to Harry. Bill listened carefully. I stopped and waited for the axe to fall when he said the most marvelous thing.

"If a woman wrote something like that to me, I would love it," he answered without hesitation.

I was stunned.

"Honestly?" I asked, one foot on Earth, one poised over the precipice.

"Honestly. I'd be thrilled."

So I thanked Bill, wrote out the e-mail and, with dizzying bravado, hit SEND while I still had the courage. Here is what I wrote.

Dear Harry,

Well, I took your advice at the lake to heart about how to handle my boss. So I'm still pretty pumped by the adrenaline rush of saying my piece unequivocally and not backing down. Which brings me to you. I have to tell you that the last morning we were at the lake, when you and I were the only ones up, and you were making scrambled eggs, and your hair was still a little tousled, you were about as appealing as a man can be. It was very hard not to say anything right then, but steeled as I am, I'm saying it now.

I think it's time for you to come to Raleigh and kiss me.

Now if I never cross your mind, or you've never thought about this, or you're not interested or not in the mood or not ready or not any number of other possibilities, that's fine, and we can just continue on as we have been. This is a no lose deal.

But if it's ever crossed your mind, it's time to cowboy up.

E

The plunge back down to Earth was immediate. I couldn't believe I'd sent it. I frantically Googled how to retrieve a ruinous e-mail.

The Holy Spirit had been working on both of us, though, and Harry was experiencing some enlightenment of his own. Two things happened that turned him completely around. First, he learned that he had bladder cancer. Treatable, but sobering nonetheless. Harry went to his lake house to recuperate from that shock where he learned of a tragedy close to home. That very morning, Harry's neighbor and the neighbor's wife were heading from their lake house back to their home in Greenville, South Carolina. Harry's neighbor was on a motorcycle riding ahead of his wife who was in their car. It was a drizzly day, and they were driving along winding, wooded backroads. They came to a sharp curve, and the wife watched her husband curve around and out of sight. When she got around the curve herself, she saw a shattering sight. Her husband had slid into the path of an oncoming semi-trailer truck and been killed on the spot. He lay on the road under his motorcycle, both crushed under the truck.

In that small lake community, word travelled fast, and Harry heard the story within hours of the accident. He was, of course, immensely saddened for his neighbor's wife. Having lost a spouse himself, his heart went out to her. But the news also had a profound effect on his view of himself and his own life. The synergy of both blows made him look at his life and say, "Life's too short. I want to go fish in Colorado and go see the Grand Canyon, and I don't want to live the rest of my life alone." On Sunday, August 31, he drove back to Charlotte with a new outlook.

That same Sunday, I had a new outlook as well. Witness protection seemed the only plausible step. The moment I hit SEND, I was aghast. I churned over that decision for the next few days until by Sunday, I was trying to come up with some kind of damage control. So I wrote Harry another e-mail about how I'd gone way out on a limb which I now deeply regretted.

Monday came and went with no response. This I was certain meant that Harry was not only *not* interested, but now he was alarmed and trying to figure out how to disentangle himself from his daughter's boss in a gracious yet decisive manner. Tuesday came and went in cyber silence, and I felt more foolish with every passing moment. Wednesday dawned with nary a word. At this point, I believed Harry was just going to respond by not responding at all. All the king's horses and all the king's men... .

Late Wednesday afternoon, after a day of blessed distraction, I signed onto my e-mail, and lo and behold, there was an e-mail from Harry. I was so afraid to open it, I just sat for several moments looking at his name in my inbox. I believed I knew what Harry's response was, but if I didn't open his e-mail, I could go on a little longer without knowing for certain. Without having to admit that everyone else was right, and I'd smashed the whole thing to smithereens.

I finally clicked open the e-mail, held my breath, and began to read. Here's how Harry started.

Thanks for the e-mail and thanks especially for your forthright message about your feelings for me. I admit that I was astonished.

My heart sank, and I had to lay my head down on my desk. I started to feel nauseated. I took a deep breath and continued reading what I thought was the last e-mail I'd ever get from him:

I regard myself as anything but appealing, but beauty is in (you know the rest). I am flattered and would "cowboy up" in an instant were I not so currently distracted.

WHAT??!! He would "cowboy up" in an instant?! I leaped from my chair, ran out of my office, stood in the middle of the hallway, and screamed at the top of my lungs,

"KAAAAAAAAAAAAY!"

My beautiful, wonderful friend, Kay Ruth, miraculously appeared at the other end of the hall. She took one look at the grin on my face and came running. We just threw our arms around each other and started laughing with relief until I finally gathered my wits enough to tell her,

"He said he'd cowboy up!"

"What else did he say?" Kay grinned still hugging me.

"I have no idea!"

So we ran back into my office, sat down at my computer, and I read the rest out loud.

As it happens, I began to notice blood in my urine on Tuesday, went to the local urologist on Thursday, had a CAT scan on Friday (normal) and a bladder inspection this morning. This inspection revealed a tumor that will be removed on Monday, September 8. These things are common in white males over the age of 50, and I am not overly concerned, but will need to get this out of the way before I come to Raleigh and kiss you. All things being equal, this I will surely do. Again, I regard myself as flattered and astonished.

Love,
H

PS: I got your e-mail today at work about the limb and your status as being off the end of it, and I was puzzled totally until I read your e-mail tonight. Well, no worries. I'm glad you went off the end of the limb. Feels good, right?

I couldn't push another sound out past the lump in my throat. I turned and looked at Kay. She couldn't speak either. All we could do was smile at each other through teary eyes.

Harry loved me.

Harry was coming to kiss me, and Harry loved me.

"You remind me of him in so many ways."
- Eileen

~ Dad ~

When I was eight years old, my mother, Val, married Frank Call, a man my grandmother called "a prince among men." Bob Acker fathered me, but Frank was my dad. Val always said that while most men who dated a woman considered a child a liability, Frank considered me a bonus. He was as anxious for children as he was for a wife, and Val used to say she sometimes wondered which of us he wanted more. It was Frank who wrote to Bob and convinced him to give up his parental rights to me, so Frank could adopt me. I always believed Bob felt relieved to be rid of me, of the obligation. When I was in college, I located Bob and went to see him with that single question. "How could you give me up?" It wasn't really a question so much as an accusation. Bob said he was moved by a letter Frank wrote to him assuring him, one father to another, that he loved me and would take care of me as his own. Bob said it was Frank's heartfelt letter that persuaded him that giving me up was the best thing for me. I dismissed Bob's answer as a self-serving lie, so I didn't believe him then, but I do now. I am able to now because Harry loved me. Harry's love healed old wounds and made my heart generous, made me forgiving.

When Frank and Val married, I assumed it was only a matter of time before he left, and Val and I were back to being on our own. I had nothing against Frank, but I was biding my time. Frank had a different view of things, though. He acted like a proud papa, teaching me to ride a two-wheeler, taking me to see the Milwaukee Braves, holding up the phone so his own father could listen long-distance to me playing "Julida Polka" on the accordion. I did not know what to make of him.

I know now. Did you ever see one of those plastic-ridged pictures that is a different picture depending on which way you tilt your head? That's called a lenticular image. That's what God gave me in Dad, a long, lenticular look at my life. It was years before I learned to tilt my head to see the other image, but when I did, the resemblance moved me to tears. This way Dad, that way Harry, this way Dad, that way Harry.

One night, I couldn't sleep, so I got up and wrote this to Harry.

I want to keep talking to you tonight, and you make me want to open up to you, so in an attempt to get to sleep and stay asleep (meaning not waking up every hour thinking about you), I'm going to turn our attention from our recent palpitating topics and tell you about my dad. There will not be a quiz, so you can bail any time here. And yes, English major that I am, I'm going to subject you to a poem I wrote about him, but only to make a point. So if you're still reading, don't say you didn't know what you were getting into.

My mother was engaged to a young doctor during World War II, but he was killed in the war. She was so distraught and bereft that she chose to marry the first man who made her laugh. He turned out to be not so funny, and she left him when I was three. For several years, she swore off dating. She and my dad were both working at Caterpillar in Milwaukee at the time, and he was chosen to head up a big project and told to choose his staff. He chose her and worked on her for two solid years to get her to go out with him. She wouldn't budge until a mutual friend put them together in a company golf tournament, and that was that. When he proposed to her, it was a two-parter. First, he asked whether she would marry him. When she said, "Yes," he said,

"Good, now is it all right with you if I adopt Eileen?" Astounded, she again said yes, to which he replied, "Good because I've already talked to my lawyer, and here's what we need to do." Frank had everything worked out, and he was the one who convinced my biological father to give up his parental rights. Though he and my mother had two daughters of their own, he treated all three of us the same. The highest praise I can give you is to tell you you remind me of him in so many ways. That's a compliment I've never given any other man in my life. He was the rock of the family. My mother suffered from depression and her emotions went up and down, but he was always the same sweet, funny, tenderhearted man every day. He was also a very spiritual person, though he never talked about these things. He was the one who got us all to church because for most of his adult life, he believed that the church was the best place from which to bring about social change. In his way, he also tried to lead a holy life. The only two foods he couldn't abide were Spam (from his Army days) and tomato soup. I didn't know this until after his death, but once a week he would force himself to go to the cafeteria at work and eat tomato soup. He thought that everything was provided by God and was therefore good, and that we should be thankful even if it wasn't quite to our liking. So he made this weekly act of thanksgiving. In World War II, he was a medic first in Italy and then in Africa where they were chasing Rommel all over the desert. He saw a lot of hunger and determined that no one around him would ever be hungry. This pledge he raised to an art form. The best example was one Sunday when he, my mother, my sisters, my aunt and uncle, and I were all riding along in Cleveland when we passed by Dad's favorite bakery. He suggested that we stop and get some cookies, so we all trooped into the bakery together. While we were looking over the cookies, Dad was milling amongst us asking which ones each of us liked. We thought he was trying to find ones that we all agreed on, but when he finally ordered, he got each of us our own dozen of the kind we wanted. We paraded out, each carrying our own little, string-tied box of cookies, eight dozen in all.

I miss him every day. I know it's only because of knowing him that I can even imagine a kind and merciful Father/God. Here is the afore-threatened poem. It explains him better than I can right now.

Kid

My father used to call me Kid.
His natural daughters he called by countless nicknames,
Liz, Liza Beth, Lauraliz,
Kissy, Chrissalee, Chrissydee,
But I was always Kid.

I was eight when he courted my mother.
I thought he was a gangster.
He wore a hat and drove a two-tone Buick
with snazzy red upholstery.
I watched The Untouchables.
I knew only outlaws wore those dapper clothes
and drove such flashy cars.

But he made good pancakes
and knew the words to any song I named.
One night, he sat at the foot of my bed,
half singing, half reciting all the verses
to my favorite Johnny Mercer ballad
while I wrote down every word
in my newly perfect cursive.

Saturday nights, we all stepped out at Howard Johnson's.
Dad and I ate steamy Indian pudding
as my mother and sisters shook their heads.
Late into the night, the others gone to bed,
we stayed up watching Alfred Hitchcock,
me on the floor as close to the sanctuary of his chair
as I could get without appearing cowardly.

When I was sixteen,
Dad took me and my best friend along on a business trip
So we could see a nearby college.
It was the night the Beatles were on Ed Sullivan.
I planned to marry Paul,

and my friend was going to marry John.
She was so overcome that night,
she broke a slat jumping up and down on the hotel bed.

The next night, as we rode back home,
A Beatles marathon resounded on the radio,
And this respectable Republican and his giddy passengers
Caroled "P.S. I Love You,"
Holy as a hymn,
As we drove into the dark.

The day before I left for college, I got a postcard,
the only mail he ever sent to anyone apart from The War.
From a hotel room on the road,
he jotted in his sparse, efficient hand,
"Good luck, Kid."

I never heard him shout.
My mother heard him only once,
a story she recounted only after he was dead.
He'd argued with his sister over their father's will.
She begrudged my small bequest because I wasn't blood.
And for the only time anyone recalled,
He raged,
Spending his single anger defending me,
Defending us.

Some months into his cancer, I wrote him how I felt,
like a note stuffed into a bottle,
a hapless china ship bobbing out to sea.
He never wrote back,
never spoke of it,
never even said he got it.
Years later, packing up his things,
I found the folded, yellowed letter in his dresser drawer
Secreted among his boxer shorts and socks.
Near the end, he asked one day if I would drive him into work.
His good blue suit engulfed him

like tarpaulin over scaffolding.
He leaned against the car door
staring silently out the window,
But he strode into his office
like a cowboy back on the range.
His secretary sized me up, then christened,
"She's certainly your daughter. She looks just like you."
And he raised his eyes from important papers,
Crooked his old-self, gamin grin at me, and mused,
"Think so?"
And we smiled a way
We never had before.

The last hours of his life,
his soul still tethered to his body
by a tangle of tubes beside the bed,
he lay beyond our reach.
I sat beside him helplessly stroking his hand.
All my words were gone,
but I leaned so close, my lips just brushed his ear
and whispered, pleading as a prayer,
"Dad, it's me. I love you."
And caressing as a kiss,
his eyelids fluttered, as if for just a moment,
he looked back from where he was going
and smiled his beauty smile,
at the daughter he chose,
the daughter who chose him,
his kid.

Dad and me, 1973

"Do not let your smile fade until I can make it permanent."
- Harry

~ The Big Smack ~

God has a sense of humor. In kindergarten one day when I was five years old, the teacher asked each of us to get up and sing a little song. Any song we wanted. One by one, each of my classmates reluctantly shuffled to the front of the class and shyly sang, "Little Duckie Duddle," "Teddy Bear's Picnic," "Big Rock Candy Mountain," and so on. All very sweet, but when my mother and I sang, we were always in the car, radio blaring, singing along with Rosemary Clooney, Frankie Laine, Gogi Grant, Nat King Cole... . By five years old, I had quite a repertoire. So when I was called up last, I walked to the front of the class and confidently belted out "Kiss of Fire" with special emphasis on the heart rending, "I know I must surrender to your kiss of fire!" Stopped the show. I look back now and see God winking,

"You'll *really* get the punchline down the road."

After reading Harry's response to my "cowboy up" e-mail, I drove home in a daze. Later that night, after dinner, I sat down and answered him.

63

What a relief! It does indeed feel wonderful to have fallen off that limb. Ever since we had coffee in Charlotte, and you looked so good and were so funny and charming, there's been a huge discrepancy between what I've said and what I've wanted to say, and I've felt like I was tripping over my tongue. Part of your considerable charm and appeal is that you don't even realize how wonderful you really are.

Right now, with your bladder surgery in the offing, you are surely the one in need of kissing, and were I able to arrange it, I would come to you. How long is the recovery for this kind of surgery? Do you have to go under general anesthetic or can they do an epidural or something like that? And is this something they can do with laparoscopy or is it more invasive? I trust your assessment of the situation, but I wish I could be there with you, so you could see me smiling at you. Here's a thought that might "distract" you in a happier way on Monday and that you might like to hear. You are always in my head. Always. Whether I'm talking to a student, arguing with my boss, playing my cello, or just waking up in the middle of the night, you're always there. It's dizzying to be able to finally say that. It feels like a gift.

Love,
E

15 minutes later, Harry wrote back.

First, let me assure you that I am not wonderful. I am an engineer. Engineers, by definition, are more interested in things than they are people. In consequence, I share with my brother (and a few sister) engineers the annoying trait of being pretty oblivious to the human dynamic and drama that is playing out around them. I didn't divine your feelings at all.

As for the operation, I will have general anesthetic. This because the doc wants me to be absolutely still while he scrapes away at this "thing" that has taken root in my bladder. I want to be perfectly still, too, and even more, don't want to make small talk with the doc while he works. The deal is that I go in on Monday and will be out on Tuesday. No cutting of the skin is involved, so I leave it to you to imagine how it is that they access the bladder.

I had a long phone conversation with Jen this morning. With respect to your e-mail and my response, I was mum. She probed, but I remained mute. My thought is that when both of us are sure that there is something she needs to know, we should both tell her. I love my Jen and don't want her to be subject to emotional overload. She thinks the world of you and loves me as her Dad. I don't want to mess this up. One final note. Never in my life have I met a seventeen-year-old person as poised as Phaedra. I don't know how the two of you did it, but Phaedra is surely wonderful. Not once, for example, did she say "like". Amazing.

Love,
H

The next morning, I answered,

As I read your e-mail, my cheeks are still hurting from sustaining this smile I've been smiling ever since I read your earlier email. Let me assure you that I have a mind of my own, and you are most definitely wonderful, engineering traits included. I did begin to catch on that, reserved and reticent as I can be, with you, I was right in there with the champ. Which is when I dropped off the limb.

The surgery. This sounds more elaborate than it did before. If I were having surgery, it would be very comforting to have you there. Now I know you are a very manly man who has been doing just fine for a long time on his own, and who can take care of himself very well indeed. And I know your brother and his wife will probably be there with you, and I concede it might give them pause if I were there and you had to explain my presence with, "This is Eileen. She's waiting for me to come out of the anesthetic and kiss her." But I would like to support you in this and do whatever would help you the most. So if there's any part of you that would like me to be there, I'm there - gladly.

65

Hospitals are my strong suit.

Love,
E

I was not being glib. My dad had suffered for six years with cancer, my mother for two. I was good at hospitals. The next morning before work, Harry wrote,

Thanks for the e-mail and for the offer to come and support me in this. As it happens, this kind of thing is entirely unsupportable. By this I mean that all of the action takes place when I am unconscious and have, really, nothing to do with it. My brother and sister-in-law will indeed be there to listen to me carp after the thing is done, but really, it's nothing that I would want to subject you to.

I am taking a vacation day tomorrow and will spend the weekend at the lake fishing, fooling with my bamboo rod project and generally enjoying the place. I seem to never tire of being there.

I am looking within myself for the wonderful part, but so far, nothing.

Love,
H

While Harry was incommunicado at the lake, I e-mailed him a forthright, unabashed history of my terrible life decisions and their domino effect. Harry returned home a day early from the lake and replied,

Thanks for the e-mails, your forthrightness, and your incredible overestimation of my appeal. I do appreciate the misery that your marriage created and the feeling of being filled with concrete is a perfectly apt phrase. That you have risen above all of this is a testament to the human (your) spirit. I'm still coming to Raleigh to kiss you. However, I don't know exactly when. With

66

luck, next weekend. As regards impure thoughts, I no longer believe in them. That is, thoughts are just thoughts, and all of us humans have, more or less, thoughts of all kinds, both noble and base. We can't help it, I think. Actions are a different matter altogether. Finally, should I make it to Raleigh next weekend, be careful with me. I will have just suffered some pretty serious abuse and will be unable to tolerate much excitement.

Finally, thanks again for telling me everything you think I need to know. I didn't actually need to know, but I do think that you needed to tell me.

Love,
H

Late that afternoon, I answered,

Sunday - unless we're being lambasted by Hurricane Isabel. Phaedra tells me they're thinking it will likely hit NC next weekend, including Raleigh, and be worse than Fran was. So this leaves only e-mail in the meantime as the means to flirt with you. Alrighty then. I'll tell you this. While you've been in the hospital and at home recovering, you've been having a very interesting effect on the people at school. It seems you are written all over my face, and the smile I keep smiling appears to be something of a force of nature. I'll be standing at the copier just coming out of a daydream about you to find some man standing there smiling back at me. One guy friend of mine today just came right out with it and said, "Ok, what's going on with you? You look way too happy to be working here." I hope this is what you're going for be-cause the ship has sailed, and this is what you've got.

Harry answered early the next morning.

Thanks for the e-mail and for the interesting story on the effect of your smile on those around you. I am glad to be the cause of such a positive effect. Here in Charlotte, the picture is different. I spent the entire day in more or less one chair trying to read and dreading the next call of nature. In brief, it still

hurts to pee. Thinking of you causes a grimace. Let me explain. When I think
of you and the promised kiss, as I have a hundred times today, nature takes
it's course, and as it does, I am rewarded with exquisite pain. Romantic, eh?
Even so, there it is.

Do not let your smile fade until I can make it permanent.

Early one morning before starting my work day, I wrote,

I am sitting at my desk looking like the picture of dedication working on a
report that is due tomorrow, but actually thinking only and completely about
you. I have got to find a way to wedge something else into my mind, but I
have no idea how to accomplish that. I'm afraid it's going to take a realign-
ment of the planets. Maybe writing to you will help – for a while at least. In
the English countryside in the 1800s, they used to run the mail 5 times a day
because people wrote so voraciously and voluminously to each other. Now I
understand. You say you are not overly concerned, but I find I'm nervous as
I wait for Jen to call and relay what the pathology report says. The synergy of
your surgery and the fast approaching hurricane is starting to paint a star
crossed hue over our situation. Apparently my smile is still intact, however.
This morning a fellow who works for me told me I was glowing. It's all you.
You cannot get here fast enough.

September 23, 2003, was the big day. In the wee hours of that morning, I still hadn't been able to get to sleep. I knew what Harry's arrival
meant. I had an overwhelming sensation of being led along by the
hand, and I knew - *I KNEW* - that if this was any kind of a decent kiss,
we would get married. Harry later told me that he had the same sensation. We were at the threshold of a transformation. Everything
would be different. So I couldn't sleep. At about 2 a.m., I got out of
bed, went to my desk , sat looking at the computer. I finally e-mailed,

I can't sleep.

Nothing more. I was certain Harry was sleeping soundly, and all I really wanted was to send that little note into the void. But as I sat there, a couple minutes later came,

Neither can I.

I touched the words on the screen and felt like Harry was right there with me already. I turned off the computer and barely got back into bed before falling fast asleep.

At about 1:00 in the afternoon, my cowboy finally arrived. I watched his Highlander pull into the driveway and went shakily out to meet him. We met each other on the sidewalk in front of my house, threw our arms around each other, and finally had what my sister, Christie, later dubbed "The Big Smack."

I had not listed "really good kisser" as one of the criteria I presented to God. God threw that in as a signing bonus.

Harry later told me, "I could feel all this love just gushing out from you, and I said to myself, 'I need that. I want that.'" We dizzily staggered into the house, and after about 15 minutes, Harry grinned and said,

"You love me, don't you." A question, but he said it as a fact.

I could barely speak, so I just nodded.

"I love you, too. Could we just skip over the two years of me coming every weekend to take you to a movie, and just go ahead and get married? I know you and you know me. Could we just get married?"

There was only one possible answer.

Say it with me.

Yes.

Newly engaged

"I am terrified for you."
- Harry

~ Foreshadow ~

The night of the Big Smack, as soon as Harry got back to Charlotte, he called me to tell me he loved me, and to tell me an extraordinary thing. He told me that he had not prayed in the ten years since his wife's funeral, but that for the two and a half hour drive back to Charlotte, he kept begging God over and over,

"Please don't let her die. Please don't let her die."

Harry had come back to life, and he ran straight back to God.

Monday morning after the Big Smack, Harry's daughter Jennifer called me from New York City. Harry had phoned all his family the night before and told them he was getting married. He wasn't looking for approval; he was just giving them the news. He'd also told everyone he was going to buy me an engagement ring that week. Jennifer was calling to ask what kind of ring design appealed to me. She assumed Harry would call and ask her for advice on what kind of ring to buy, so she wanted to be prepared.

71

Harry had other plans, however, and they did not involve anyone but him and me. He had all the confidence in the world and didn't need anyone else's opinion. He knew what he wanted. He wanted to come back with a big rock in hand. Then he wanted to get married as soon as possible.

Moments after I hung up from talking with Jennifer, Harry himself called from a jewelry store in Charlotte where he'd already picked out a ring. His only question for me was whether I liked white or yellow gold. Surprised that he'd handled this so quickly, I asked whether he had talked with Jennifer yet that morning. He said no. He was barreling ahead as if he and I were the only ones in the world. I liked that. I liked that a lot.

Monday night, we talked. Endlessly. A conversation that only the crazy in love could find fascinating. I will not bore you with it. I'll only add that Tuesday night, we had the same identical conversation, and I was riveted. So was Harry.

Wednesday morning, however, brought us to a crossroads. The phone was already ringing as I unlocked my office. It was Harry. He said he'd had a terrible night, and that he wasn't sure whether it was fair to me for him to marry me. He said he wanted to marry me, but only if he were cancer free. He understood very well the role of the helpless witness. He had been through that already and said he didn't want to put me through it. My poor, sweet man was on the horns of a dilemma, but I thought there was something more important here than just my reaffirming my commitment to him no matter what. I told him that I wasn't sure that I could marry *him* if he didn't understand what we were really signing up for. He had thought he was being unselfish and found my stand a little perplexing. I asked him whether he had ever seen the movie or read the book *Shadowlands*. *Shadowlands* is the true story of writer and theologian C.S. Lewis and the love and commitment that grew between him and poet Joy

72

Gresham precisely because of, not in spite of, her terminal illness. Harry said he'd never heard of it, so I told him to go rent the movie and then call me after he had watched it. He said he would and that he loved me, and we hung up. I immediately sat down and e-mailed him the following:

Dear man I love,

Your attempts at retraining me to always communicate with you are starting to bear fruit. I am going to tell you about this morning. Saying that you didn't want to marry me if you were dying of cancer launched us into the most important discussion we may ever have in our lives. This is how I see it. A commitment with conditions, however selfless they may be, is not a real commitment. I want to live a holy life. I want to live in God's will. When I found out you had cancer, I saw that God was showing us at least a glimpse of His plan, and I promised Him that I would do whatever is in His plan. I promised Him.

You and I are in a holy plan. The consummation of that plan is not our wedding night, it is our marriage. The Sacrament of Marriage. Sacrament.

You have spent most of your life being the daddy and taking care of everyone else. You have done your job absolutely superbly. But now it's time for you to really understand the importance and beauty of your completely letting go of everything and living in God's plan. The first words that our dear John Paul II said as Pope were, "Be not afraid."

Be not afraid. I love you.

It seemed as if I had barely hit SEND when Harry called me again from work. This time, he had a new opener.

"Hello, my loveperson/wife."

"We're not even married yet. I'm 'wife' already?"

"Yup. I get it now." He was quiet for a moment and then he said,

"I never heard anybody say that before in my life."

"What?"

"I want to live a holy life," as if he were speaking Swahili with no idea what he was saying.

Later that afternoon, he e-mailed,

I do so deeply regret my thoughtlessness. No sooner had I hung up the phone than I realized that married or not, you will suffer if I do. My thought to spare you from setting sail on a sinking ship was, of course, stupid. The ship has sailed, and I am so glad to be on it with you.

I got the movie (which was only available on dvd). I will watch it tomorrow and will be moved, I am sure. From reading the jacket, I think that I already understand the message. I know that I have for a long time protected myself from further harm by keeping the world at arm's length. You changed that, and now I am as vulnerable as I was when first I married.

Please don't get sick. Please drive carefully. Please don't do stupid things while high on coffee.

Actually, I am completely unafraid for myself. I am terrified for you.

Love,
H

"This is the Olympics of marriage."
- Harry

~ Shock and Awe ~

God's plans are seldom meant only for the one who prayed. God loves economy. Something for everyone. One stone, many birds.

The weekend after The Big Smack, Harry made his triumphant return to Raleigh. I was anxiously waiting outside on the porch swing when I saw his Highlander coming down the street. I went down to the historic sidewalk to meet him, and all we could do was hug each other and grin. We went inside, and Harry called to Phaedra. When she came out, he asked us to sit down on the couch next to each other. We had no idea what he was up to, but we sat down. He stood in front of us, beaming away, reached into his pocket, and brought out a black ring box. Stepping forward, he leaned over, handed the box to Phaedra, and asked,

"Phaedra, would you please give this to your mother?"

He then straightened up, put his hands behind his back, and beamed. He was loving us all being together in that moment, all being together in that adventure. Phaedra was a little perplexed, but she handed the box to me. Clearly, Harry had a plan, so I just smiled back at him, waiting for him to tell me what came next. He beamed at me for a moment, and then said,

"Now would you please open the box?"

I slowly opened the box and saw a dazzling, round, brilliant cut solitaire diamond set in white gold. It was exactly like the ring Dad had presented to my mother, but twice the size. I was speechless. I looked up at Harry who was now beaming broadly.

"Do you like it?" he asked, eyes sparkling.

I had never seen anything so beautiful or extravagant. All I could do was nod.

With the naïveté of the crazy in love, we assumed that since we were so happy, everyone else would be happy for us as well, and for the most part, that was true. Our story rapidly became legend, one person passing it along to another, passing on hope to those who had been looking for love. My sisters had watched me struggle through years of family upheaval and heartache, and they badly wanted to see me happy. Still stunned by the sudden turn of events, they nonetheless suspended disbelief and took Harry in with open hearts. I close my eyes and can still see my sister Christie, her husband Rob, and Harry and I sitting around their kitchen table, jubilant and joking, marveling at how surprising life can be. I can still hear Harry telling them,

"This is the Olympics of marriage, and I'm going for gold."

Later, Christie e-mailed me 'The Harry Report".

What a wonderful man has come into your, and by extension our, lives. Although we only visited for a short time, Rob and I liked him immediately. I think he is intelligent, funny, engaging, charming, compassionate, and even

somewhat charismatic. In short, I think you have yourself a real winner there. Did you know he wrote me a very nice e-mail thanking me for a warm welcome? And the ring is truly beautiful. Not that it matters when the man who gave it to you is so beautiful himself.

I love you,
Christie

I passed this happy assessment on to Harry, and he wrote,

Your sister is a peach. I liked her, and I liked Rob immediately, too. A wonderful family. I look forward to the 17th.

You called me from work at 5:01 PM. I was cleaning the bathtub at the time and missed your call. It is now 6:18 p.m., and I am as anxious as a teenager about when you will try me again. I am here and waiting for the phone to ring.

How totally goofy I am.

Love,
H

My sister Laura drove up from Florida with her daughters, Chelsie and Scarlett, greeting Harry with a warm hug and effusive, "Harry, my brother!" while Chelsie and Scarlett memorialized The Big Smack in sidewalk chalk. Harry's brothers had also seen him through some dark times, and they were delighted to hear the news, his brother, Don, later telling me, "Thank you for giving us back our brother." When Harry took me to Charlotte to meet his twin brother, Larry, Larry's wife Donna, gave me some insight into how singular and surprising Harry's actions were when she confided, "Harry didn't even ask anyone's opinion this time. He just did it," raising her eyebrows meaningfully at me. This was apparently unusual.

Though our siblings were happy, all this elation was lost on some of our children. Parents are perplexing, after all. They are some of the only people in our lives that we address by role rather than by name. It can take many years, many life experiences, to stop looking at what happens to our parents in terms of how it affects us, rather than how it affects them. My youngest daughter, Phaedra, liked Harry the first time they met, and she had predicted way back in February that we were destined to marry, so she was happy but not surprised. My older daughter, Jessamin, liked Harry from the start as well, and later revealed to me that she was actually relieved we were marrying, saying, "Now I don't have to worry about you anymore." The night Harry called and told everyone we were engaged, his youngest daughter, Jill, sat right down and wrote me a heartfelt, lovely letter saying, "I love you already." But Harry's two oldest children, John and Jennifer, were another matter.

The Saturday after Harry came back to Raleigh with the ring, he and I flew up to New York City, so I could meet his son, John and his wife, Emily. Since Harry's daughter Jennifer had introduced us and pushed us together, we were confident of her support, and Harry believed Jennifer's matchmaking role would convince John that I was going to be a good addition to the family. We were wrong on all fronts. You might have seen this coming, but we didn't.

We were supposed to first go to Jennifer's studio apartment and then all go meet John and Emily for lunch. We took a taxi from JFK to Jennifer's, expecting to be greeted with teary hugs and smiles. But when Jennifer opened the door, she greeted us coolly, sat us both down on her small futon couch, pulled up a chair in front of us, and began scolding,

"I don't know either one of you!"

Stunned, we looked at Jennifer, glanced quizzically at each other, and turned blankly back to Jennifer, not knowing what to say.

"What do you mean?" Harry finally asked bewilderedly.

"What are you thinking getting married?!" she yelled back.

More confusion.

"What do you mean?" Harry asked, perplexed, "You're the one who got us together."

"But I didn't know THIS would happen!" Jennifer chided.

"What did you think would happen?" Harry asked, smiling slightly.

"I thought you'd date for a couple years! Get to know each other! You don't even know each other!" Jennifer rebuked.

"We know everything we need to know," Harry assured her, taking my hand.

Jennifer was not reassured.

"You haven't even had your first fight yet!" she shouted.

"I'm not going to fight with her," Harry said as we grinned, starry-eyed, at each other, and shook our heads.

"Me either," I finally weighed in.

This back and forth went on awhile longer, until Jennifer finally said,

"We have to go meet John and Em, but we're not done talking about this," and ushered us out the door.

At the restaurant, John greeted me cordially with a handshake. We all sat down and ordered, and then Emily asked how we had gotten together. This was our favorite story, and Harry liked me to tell it, so I came right out with the truth. Told them how I'd prayed, how Jennifer had come into my office two days later, all of it. I wanted them to see God's handiwork.

But God was not their focus, and John asked to speak to his father alone. So Harry and John went off for a little walk, and Emily and I made small talk while Jennifer sat in silence.

After Harry and John returned, the five of us strolled around Manhattan, going in and out of bookstores, getting coffee, and generally giving Harry's kids a chance to hang back with him and try to convince him he'd gone off the deep end. I found this all unexpected and unsettling. I'd already heard the story about the impact of Jennifer's opinion on Harry's decision to break things off with the woman he'd formerly been with, but Harry remained calm and undeterred. We finally stopped for dinner at a little Mexican restaurant thinking things had settled down. But Jennifer was still clearly upset and again asked Harry to go outside and talk with her. Harry sat in front of the restaurant for nearly half an hour with his troubled daughter, and John several times went outside to join them. At one point, Emily smiled sympathetically at me and said, "This must be hard for you." I was so moved by her kindness, I teared up. Finally, Harry, John and Jennifer came back, and we finished our meal, John acting like nothing was going on, Jennifer completely silent.

Early Sunday morning, Harry and John went out for coffee together, and John again tried to persuade Harry to "slow down." Like Jennifer, John brought up the concerns that, "You don't know each other," and

"You don't even know how each other fights." When Harry got back to the hotel, he came to my room and told me about his and John's conversation. Harry was not swayed. He was bloody, but unbowed.

Later that morning, John and Jennifer were startled to see a side of Harry which they had not seen in years. It being Sunday, Harry understood that I planned to go to Mass. The night before, Harry asked Jennifer where there was a nearby church, and Jennifer, John, Emily, Harry and I all ended up going to Mass together Sunday morning. John and Jennifer were stunned. The last time they had seen their father at Mass was their mother's funeral. Harry was surprising them on all fronts.

After Mass, we all went to John and Emily's apartment for brunch before Harry and I had to fly back to North Carolina. Once again, there were furtive exchanges out on the balcony, first John and Harry, then Jennifer and Harry, then all three. I was not in this. I busied myself buttering bagels and nursing along cup after cup of coffee while Emily gamely tried to put the best face on the situation. Finally, everything had been said, every point had been made, every counterpoint elaborated. Everyone had weighed in, everyone had been heard.

Everyone but me.

We all sat in John and Emily's small living room, me sitting on the floor by the couch, Jennifer on the couch, Harry, John and Emily across from us. There was finally a lull, and I decided to have my say. Voice shaking, I told them,

"I can see from your point of view how sudden and suspect this is. In your place, I'd probably be skeptical, too. And I completely understand your weighing all kinds of alternative scenarios about the future. But while you're weighing all this, I'd just like to ask you to also consider the possibility that God is putting our two broken families together to heal them."

No one moved. No one spoke until finally, a beaming Harry turned to John and said,

"See? What did I tell you? Heart of gold."

What they didn't understand, what none of us understood was that Harry and I were in a race against the clock. There was still a lot to do and little time to do it in.

But we didn't know that then.

All we knew was we were dancing on the breath of God.

"Can we not just get married, go to the lake, and be in love?"
- Harry

~ A Period of Frustration ~

Do you remember the beginning of love? Maybe you're there right now. That exquisite euphoria when all you are, all you want to be, is love. You don't eat, you barely sleep. The two of you have only one topic of conversation. "I love you." All you want to hear is, "I love you." Every time you hear it, every time you say it, "I love you" is just as new and thrilling as the first time. You can't think about anything else, can't talk about anything else. If our human love mirrors God's love, then I think maybe this "snowed" period mirrors Heaven. A constant chorus of, "I love you," ebbing and flowing, back and forth, joyfully sung into God's heart and serenaded back to ours.

Our wedding date now set for January 17, 2004, Harry and I embarked on what Harry called "a period of frustration" planning our wedding, rearranging our lives, but not there yet. Harry packed up his home in Charlotte, stayed at his brother's during the week, and came to Raleigh every weekend. This constant here-now-gone lent an eerily imaginary quality to our already dreamlike delirium. Harry kept a bottle of my musk oil with him, so he could dab some under his nose through the day to assure himself that I existed. We e-mailed endlessly.

My dear heart of my heart,

I have forgotten all the droll and clever things I was going to write to you and am only thinking about the poem below which Carl Sandburg wrote to his wife when he was away. It's how I feel right now. There will be a period of frustration. I love you.

Home Thoughts

The sea rocks have a green moss.
The pine rocks have red berries.
I have memories of you.

Speak to me of how you miss me.
Tell me the hours go long and slow.
Speak to me of the drag on your heart,
The iron drag of the long days.

I know hours empty as a beggar's tin cup on a rainy day, empty as a soldier's sleeve with an arm lost.

Speak to me...

Early the next morning, Harry answered,

I know no one who could have known, found, and reproduced the Sandburg poem as an appropriate expression of sentiment. I am lucky, and I'll take it (luck) every time.

How's this for sentiment and originality:

I LOVE YOU
H

That night, he wrote again,

My love,

It is 7:14 p.m. I am drinking scotch number two and sucking on lemon drops. This is not a good combination. The skillet meal is in the skillet and so unappetizing that I may not bother to put it on a plate.

I am watching the clock go around, awaiting the magic hour when I speak to you without penalty.

How did this happen? I really don't know. Suddenly, I can't function without the sound of your voice. This sound must be frequent and must contain three words repeated endlessly. You know what they are. Prepare to say them.

I love you,
H

The next morning, he wrote,

How to say this I do not know. I love you. How is that? I wish you were here. How is that? I wonder why I am not there. How is that? I am having trouble doing my job, and it is your fault. How is that? I only avoided wrecking my car this morning because you were not walking down the sidewalk. How is that? I love you. You. You. You.

If I need to come to Wake Tech and have a fist fight with any of the boys, let me know.

Love,
H

Another evening, he wrote,

Well my love,

I have spent the entire evening fooling around with wedding e-mails and stuff to the complete neglect of my paying job, which I like less and less. This as I like you more and more.

Can we not just get married, go to the lake, and be in love?

Love,
H

After Harry left one Monday morning, I felt like he had been a mirage. Bereft, I pined,

I feel like an amputee. I can feel you, but you're not really here. Chocolate can't fix this.

When he got to work, Harry wrote back,

Well your message is/was enigmatic. Even though we talked and talked, I can only say that I WAS there, and that I am still, at least spiritually.

Night and day,
You are the one.
Only you
Beneath the moon and under the sun,
Whether near to me or far,
It makes no difference where you are,
I think of you
Night and day.

I love you. You, you, nobody but you. Verse?

H

Harry was having a similar reaction to all this back and forth himself, though, and later wrote,

I have spent the last hour waiting for some sign of life from your phone. Do you know how I love you? I think not! I have just applied musk oil to my philtrum and am thinking of you quite continuously, quite intensely, quite appropriately. You seem to me from this distance in time and space to be a dream. Call and let me know that this is not so.

Invigorated by love and hope for the future, Harry wanted to tackle his smoking habit before our wedding. He did not fit the "addictive personality" profile, but where smoking was concerned, one addiction cascaded into the next. At this point, Harry was smoking a pipe almost nonstop. He knew there was a direct correlation between smoking and bladder cancer. He sincerely wanted to quit, wanting our wedding day to be the start of a new life in every way. So he'd been talking about quitting smoking for several weeks. Late one Friday afternoon, I was sitting out on the porch when his Highlander rolled into view. I got up and started walking down the sidewalk to meet him when I saw him get out of the driver's side with something unfamiliar in his mouth. He turned around, and I saw that where his pipe had always been, there was now a fat cigar. Harry smiled broadly and threw his arms open. I had to ask, but I almost didn't want to hear the answer.

"What's that you're smoking?"

"Well, the good news is I finally quit smoking a pipe!"

"I see that. So what is this now?"

"Well, I was so happy at giving up the pipe, that I lit up a celebratory cigar and was hooked!"

The epilogue to this little story is that after we married and moved to the lake house, Harry tried to give up cigars by replacing them with hard candy, but developed such an addiction to Starlight Mints that I would wake up in the middle of the night to the smell of peppermint and the sound of Harry crunching in his sleep.

On we babbled.

Dear man of my dreams,

I just left you a phone message saying I was given free movie tickets to a preview showing for tonight, so I will be at the movies tonight. This has been a very tiring day - lots of grading and interviewing, but I got a lot done, so this is a nice reward.

I talked with my cousin Miles who will not be able to attend the wedding, but my cousin Lynn said she, my Aunt Maureen, and my cousin Rick will be driving down from NJ. I also talked to the florist. The two arrangements will total about $300.

I love you passionately, exquisitely, wholeheartedly (I love that word), unreservedly, and openarmedly (ok, I made that one up). I must go home now and feed our daughter hamburgers. Ever more hamburgers.

As the Beatles would say, "Love, love, love."

My loveperson,

You said that this email, the one to which I am responding, was nothing. Quite the contrary. Your words mean so much to me that I cannot respond adequately except to say the same old thing, which itself deserves some kind of e-mail abbreviation. Let's try ILY.

I am very glad that Maureen will make the wedding. I am likewise sorry that *the flowers will cost only $300. It seems to me that, for such an occasion and for such an amazing, wonderful event, they should cost much more. Think then about this; how much should we give Father Dougherty and Monsignor O'Connor for officiating at our wedding? Be aware that I am aware that I have spelled Dougherty in the Irish way, not in the way that he actually spells it. This is entirely his problem as he is entirely Irish, not Greek.*

How about punctuation in the above paragraph? How does one actually punctuate the question in the sentence that begins with the "Think then" stuff? I rely upon you for this information and much more. In addition, ILY.

I will say to you that, at one time in my life, I met a Nobel nominee, whose name I have blissfully forgotten, who gave me one of his notable papers to read. In this paper, he repeatedly cited himself as: "Name (the guy's name, blissfully forgotten), personal communication." Ego? I am so glad to have you as my wife and to have left my ego behind me, like Louis Armstrong's excrement. The Louis reference is in a book on the shelf at the lake. Originally, I had written this last sentence in parentheses. Having somewhere read that parentheses were the crutch of weak writers, I changed it. All this because ILY and care about your red pencil.

Wholeheartedly your own dear man person,

ILY really Quite Enormously (ILYRQE). (This would be a really good password!)

Later that evening, he wrote,

My dear sweet cello, loveperson, woman,

It is not 5:30 p.m. (Ask yourself; how many people know that p.m. must have the periods? Gosh, I hope that the semicolon following "yourself" is correct. Can you not see what fun we will have? I did see you reading Safire in the Sunday Times. I waited for a comment. Alas, none came. Safire's book is on

*the shelf at the lake.) The cable guy has yet to come and take away my mo-
dem, so I am frantically trying to communicate with you before he does. Con-
trast this with the time when I was in college as an undergraduate, when a
long distance phone call cost so much that once a week was extravagant. (My
parents called Erie, PA, where my Dad's family lived, exactly once a year, on
Christmas Eve.) Compare this to the article you read in the Times Magazine.
This and the rest of The Times went into the dumpster here in Charlotte
when I realized the time for romance, dalliances with lattes, discussion of
delicate writing of the literate sort, could wait for after.*

After what?

You know.

Harry was immediately and wholeheartedly committed to us as a
family, to us and our five children as a family. We had been through
some initial resistance, but we were both committed to working
things out together, not as "your children" and "my children", but as
"our children." He was especially concerned about his son, John, and
so one morning I shared this with him:

My dear man,

*I'm not quite on the clock here yet, and I was thinking about John as I drove
in this morning and so wanted to tell you this. Clearly the dear boy is in
some pain born of a misconception he has about the height and breadth of
love. He really has himself on the horns of a true dilemma. "Dad's being
alone the rest of his life is a bad thing, but Dad's being so happy and in love
is an equally bad thing. Because what does it mean if Dad is so in love? Love
can only be finite and proportional. If you give some here, you must take
some from there to have it to give. So the love Dad is feeling had to come from
somewhere else, and that somewhere else is from Mom." I think it's very
common for people who have not yet had children to believe that love is
measurable. I think it really takes both the experience of that hyperlove you*

have for your first child along with having that second child and seeing that, incredibly, you love this other little person just as much as the first before you really start understanding the unboundedness of love. I don't know how John reacted to the other woman you were with, but I would bet that in many ways, he was more comfortable with your relationship with her because it in no way "rivaled" your love for his mother. So you had companionship, but it did not take anything away from his mother in his mind. I wonder whether in some way you were struggling with this very notion yourself after you and I met. You've said you were afraid, but you haven't been able to say of what. Maybe you were wrestling with John's dilemma - if I really fall in love, what will that do/mean about my love for Janet? You had already run the experiment of companionship without love and felt that debased your memory of Janet. Maybe actually being in love would be even worse. You hadn't really run that experiment yet. So you stayed in the cave and only came out to go to the opera with Sylvia, an apparently safe choice.

So here's what I suggest. Tell all this to John man to man. Tell him you were afraid for the same reasons he is now afraid. But tell him, too, about how it was to have a relationship without love and how you felt that settling for just a "passenger" in the seat next to you without love defiled the memory of his mother. Tell him that you've found that the only true tribute to and ongoing recognition of your love for his mother is your wanting and needing love again in your life and for the rest of your life. That she herself created that need in you by making you feel completely loved and treasured.

You said you wish you and Janet had shown more of yourselves to your kids. Let John see you now. It will show him not only the man he's trying to emulate, but also the loving mother he's pining for and what she wants for both of you.

And all this on just one cup of coffee.

I love you unboundedly.

Harry answered not long after.

Wow!

Your analysis is exactly right, I think. As I read and reread your email, I marvel at the depth of your thoughts and analysis. I will speak with John privately over Thanksgiving, and see if I can make better sense of his thinking. I will also use your suggestion and get him to see me more clearly. I think that he still sees me with a child's eyes.

Well, from here on, I'll do the chores and manage the money while you teach me how to think about more important stuff. I immediately recognized the correctness of your suggestion for the Thanksgiving dilemma that I was somewhat ashamed at not having come up with it myself. I didn't want to walk away from you and Phaedra on that holiday, of course, but couldn't come up with the rationale that you did.

Please talk with Phaedra. Her alarm went off at 4:30 this morning, and she was up very late. She seemed tired, and maybe I am the cause somehow. Anyhow, were she my kid, and she is, I would be worried.

Love,
H

The engineer in Harry was also anticipating how we would navigate our life together. One night in Raleigh, we were sitting on the front porch swing, and he told me,

"Whenever we have a problem, we should run to it. Not put it off. We should run to it, so it doesn't get any bigger."

"How will we do that?" I asked somewhat hesitantly.

"Whenever there's a problem, we'll stop whatever we're doing, go lie down on the bed, put our arms around each other, and talk it out. It'll be very hard to be angry nose to nose."

More incredibly, though, one night, Harry said something in a voice that told me he'd been thinking about it for awhile. We were lying on the couch with my head on his shoulder, arm over his chest, when he put his hand over mine and said,

"We're so fortunate to be gushing with all this love. Now we need to let all this love overflow onto everyone else we love and help make their lives better."

In my entire life, I'd never heard anyone say such a thing. I'd heard people talk about giving back from the plenty they'd been given, but I'd never heard anyone talk about multiplying love, giving back love. I was absolutely awed and fell in love with him all over again.

Whenever I told Harry about my prayer and about how I believed God put us together, he always looked a little mystified. If I asked him if he believed that's how we came together, he'd say no. However, if the effect proves the cause, there was no denying the effect on him and on us.

First, Harry had prayed right after The Big Smack.

Now he believed we had a mission.

Love.

"We won't move here until you're ready."
- Harry

~ Christmas at the Lake ~

Our traditions feel like home, especially at Christmas. Foods, songs, decorations, and customs are passed on from one generation to the next and make us feel connected. Grounded. Their absence can have the opposite effect.

Harry and I had spent Thanksgiving apart to allow his children to have the holiday they had planned, but we missed each other with the heartsick longing of the newly in love. So we decided we would spend Christmas together no matter what. Harry's three kids were all coming to his lake house for the holidays, and Harry asked me and Phaedra to come join them there. Harry was very attentive to his children's feelings and was all too aware that John and Jennifer were still hesitant about our marrying. He wanted to be with me at Christmas, but he also wanted to show them that I was no threat, so in deference to his kids, he asked me essentially to be a spectator, to let them do Christmas their way without trying to introduce any of my own family traditions. At that point, Harry cared nothing for the religious meaning of Christmas, but he cared deeply about making us all into a family.

Phaedra and I arrived at Harry's lake house the afternoon of Christmas Eve. Harry had beautifully decorated the house inside and out with things from Christmases past. Garlands with big red bows hanging from the second and third level railings. Wreaths with Christmas bells above the mantel and on the doors. Colored lights wound all along the railings on the front, back and sides of the house. Illuminated icicles dangling from the eves. An enormous tree heavy with handmade ornaments lovingly crafted by children's hands, crocheted ornaments with his parents' pictures, trinkets from their travels. On the mantel, statues from the Netherlands of Sinterklaas and his trusty servant Zwarte Piet, and oversized, wooden soldier nutcrackers from Germany. A sideboard shrine of an elaborate Christmas village of cottages, churches, carolers, stores, sleighs and skaters, all the pieces his children's mother had collected.

Memorials everywhere, but not a nod to God. Nowhere was there a creche, a manger, a wise man, a shepherd, or a baby Jesus. Nowhere was there any hint that Christmas had anything to do with Christ. The highest reverence was paid to a tiny, fragile, ceramic swan swimming on a little mirror pond. This hallowed, family relic was their embodiment of Christmas.

Harry was generous with his family, and under the tree was a knee-deep mountain of presents. IPods for everyone, clothes, books, jewelry galore, and this year's traditional family sweater in eight identically wrapped boxes. From the mantel hung eight stockings stuffed with gag gifts, baubles, soaps, candles, and above all, money. Harry was in his glory. The more family, the better.

The theme of the holiday was relaxation. Everyone was assumed to be exhausted and in bad need of downtime. Meals were self-serve, everyone making their own soup, sandwich, macaroni and cheese, etc. whenever they felt like eating. The prevailing sentiment was that putting a communal meal together was hard work, and no one needed or wanted that kind of responsibility. There was, however, lots of camaraderie, lots of sitting by the fire talking or reading. Harry had little musical ability, but John was the drummer in a rock band that had a large following, mainly in Europe. Phaedra was also a talented musician. Christmas afternoon, without saying a word, Harry sat down on the couch with a guitar and started idly strumming away. When either John or Phaedra happened by, Harry would say, "Show me how to play D major again," or "What are the chords for that song 'Blow Up Your TV?'" or whatever other little enticement he could think of. I marveled as little by little, he lured each of them into the living room, first standing, then sitting, offering him their expertise. All his coaxing and cajoling finally paid off, as finally, there sat John and Phaedra, each with a guitar, laughing and playing first one song, then another. I bent down, put my arms around Harry's neck, and whispered in his ear,

"Nice work."

"And it only took me three hours," he whispered back.

I was happy to be with Harry, but the enormity of winning over all these people and of giving up my life in Raleigh and moving to this remote lake was starting to look pretty daunting. I felt as though I were moving to another country where I didn't speak the language. Life was going to be completely different. Contemplating these changes from the safety of my familiar home in Raleigh was one thing. Getting a good, up close look at them was entirely different, and I began to be afraid. I kept telling myself that I had to trust that this was all God's plan, but I was still afraid.

Harry had been going to Mass with me every weekend since we got engaged, and so on Christmas Eve, we tried to get our kids to go to midnight Mass with us but ended up going alone. Being at an unfamiliar church for Christmas where I didn't know anyone, I felt forlorn, even with Harry there. The church we went to was made from concrete blocks, even inside, and looked stark and gray. Fear had me by the throat. I didn't want to alarm Harry and tell him any of what was going on in my head, but I was overwhelmed.

Then an amazing thing happened. Have you ever been listening to a homily and heard something that seemed meant just for you? That's exactly what happened. The priest started talking about what it must have been like for Mary and Joseph traveling from Nazareth to Bethlehem. How afraid they must have been not knowing what was going to happen and not having anyone but each other. How they must have known that life was going to be completely different now and forever. Most importantly, how they finally had to just trust that they were doing what God wanted, and so for that reason, everything would be all right. God would make everything right.

I felt as if God were putting His arms around Harry and me and saying,

"Don't worry. I've got you. I know what I'm doing."

A wave of peace washed over me, and I felt enormously lifted. God had us. I knew God had us.

After Mass, Harry and I walked back to the car, hand in hand, in silence. We drove through the dark back to the lake house without speaking. When we got back, rather than turning down the driveway, Harry drove to the top of the road that overlooks the lake. Out beyond the city lights where it was just inky black, the stars were bright and brilliant. Harry put his arms around me, and we sat in silence watching a dazzling display of shooting stars. Finally, Harry spoke for the first time in nearly an hour.

"We won't move here until you're ready," he said gently.

I knew I was ready.

"You can stand behind me."
- Harry

~ Nesting ~

Harry and I were married at 11:00 a.m. on Saturday, January 17, 2004 at Our Lady of Lourdes Catholic Church in Raleigh, North Carolina. People still talk about my arrival that day. All right, they laugh about it. I am pseudo-punctual. That means I usually arrive at the stroke of the nick of time. Our wedding day was no exception. Wearing jeans and one of Harry's old shirts with my daughter, Jessamin, right behind me carefully cradling my cream colored wedding gown, I skidded into the church vestibule to find the organist blasting at full throttle and Father Dougherty, Monsignor O'Connor, four altar boys, and my tuxedoed loveperson all queued up, ready for the regal procession. Jessamin and I darted to the cry room where she helped me into my dress, and I ran back and queued up, my arm through Harry's, right behind Monsignor O'Connor. Suddenly dazed, I whispered to Monsignor,

"I can't remember anything you told us at the rehearsal last night."

"Don't worry. I'll tell you what to do," he whispered back.

There were many moments that day when my eyes welled up from pure, unadulterated joy. Watching all of our five children perform their parts in the Mass, hugging all the friends and family who had come to celebrate with us, seeing Phaedra play the banjo with the bluegrass band at the reception... . But when I reminisce about that day, the first thing I think about, the thing that brings me to tears even today, is Father Dougherty's homily about the marriage feast at Cana and how Harry and I had saved the best for last.

I was prepared for the worst. I wasn't prepared for the best. Neither of us was. We didn't know we'd fall more and more crazy in love. When I prayed asking for someone who really knew how to love a person, I didn't know God intended for me to become that person, too. For almost three years, Harry and I lived like 20-year-old newlyweds. God gave us that gift of holy and sublime bonding. He made sure we were welded together, body and soul. He had to. He was working against a deadline.

In the fall of 2004, after Phaedra was safely off to college, Harry and I moved for good to the lake in the foothills of the Blue Ridge Mountains in South Carolina. I'm going to tell you what life was like with Harry, but I give you fair warning. Once when I was telling a friend of mine some story or other about Harry, she listened with rapt attention and, though she'd never met him, sighed,

"I'm a little in love with your husband."

Guard your heart.

Harry's lake house was a unique design. Harry wanted the architecture inside and out to mirror the layered look of the foothills as they receded into the distance across the lake. The lake side of the house was floor to ceiling windows, and the roof line was three nested gables, one behind the other, each one higher than the next. Inside, the house was also on three levels, each one open to the center of the house, and all facing out so you could see the lake from every level. You could stand on the first floor and look up at the second and third floors. The top level of the house was a wonderful loft that you could only get to by climbing a library ladder with wheels that rolled along a track. The roof line was a steep A shape, so once you were up in the loft, you couldn't stand up straight, but you could see out both sides of the house to the woods behind and the lake in front. Sometimes Harry and I slept up in the loft because it felt like waking up in a huge, wonderful treehouse. Although Harry told me we could live anywhere I wanted, there was no question in my mind that we would live at the lake. For Harry, the lake and the house were paradise.

Not long after the Big Smack, Harry and I slowly began feathering our lake house nest. Things were moving fast, and we knew that in addition to planning a wedding, we had to figure out how to merge our households. At that point, Harry hadn't really done much in the way of furniture there yet. There was a leather chair and couch, and a nice oriental rug, but the rest were old odds and ends. We wanted to start fresh. So the first thing we did was buy a bed. One afternoon we were talking about what our bed should look like. Harry asked me what I wanted, and though I had always liked the look of cabin style furniture for some reason, I didn't think that was even a possibility. So I turned it back on him instead and asked what he liked. Much to my surprise, he said,

"You know, if I had my absolute druthers, I'd like a log-style bed."

"That's exactly what I want!" I laughed.

We were completely delighted and impressed with ourselves for wanting the same thing. Harry went online, and we spent a giddy couple of hours online looking at pine log beds from around the country, finally settling on a queen size bed made in northern Wisconsin to be delivered to the lake house right before Christmas. Harry clicked on "Place Your Order," pushed his chair back in triumph, and crowed,

"I'm all about the romance!"

From that jubilant triumph, we went on to order two oriental rugs on-line. The next weekend, we met in Hendersonville, North Carolina and picked out a leather chair to match the couch and chair that Harry already had. We scoured Raleigh for a love seat and chairs for the small TV room. On one excursion, we found a clever butterfly leaf dining table that could seat ten people, more if you scrunched to-gether. We bought unfinished end tables, coffee tables, and a TV armoire all of which Harry carefully, lovingly refinished himself. We picked out Tuscan designed dishes, adobe colored bath towels, and cheerily striped shower curtains. All of this we gradually moved from Raleigh to South Carolina one U-Haul load at a time.

In true engineering/manly fisherman fashion, Harry had originally painted every room in the house white. When I asked him what kinds of colors or decor he liked, he said,

"You can have anything you want. All I ask is no pink ruffles."

I love lots of color, but seeing all that white, I thought I'd better break him into the idea gradually. So I started by replacing all the standard issue silver bathroom cabinet knobs with cheery ceramic knobs painted with clay and green stripes. Harry noticed and told me they looked great, so I proceeded to replace all 33 of the boring, silver kitchen cabinet knobs with bronze, leaf-patterned knobs. By the time I was done, there was no knob left unturned. Harry was greatly amused by all this knobbing, keeping all the extra knobs in a coffee can and teasing me,

"Now whenever we travel, we'll take these with us, so you can change all the knobs in the hotel room to your little heart's delight."

The colored knobs were such a hit, I thought it was time to tackle the walls. Harry was still a little leery. Sitting in a restaurant one after-noon, we were talking about wall colors for our bedroom, when I looked up and noticed the restaurant walls were painted a very soothing latte color. I pointed this out to Harry, and we immediately decided it would look great in our bedroom. We stopped at Lowe's, bought a couple buckets of a manly, cowboyish color called Chuck Wagon, and set about painting our bedroom the very next day. Over time, Harry and I painted every wall in that house ourselves. We put on some Ray Charles, Willie Nelson, Beach Boys, or The Mamas and the Papas, and Harry did all the edging, while I did all the rolling. Harry was so delighted with the way the bedroom turned out that in no time at all, we progressed to a Tuscan gold in the open dining room/ living room area, and mossy green in the TV room. Harry was so happy with the change in the way it looked and felt inside that he told me happily,

"I trust you now. Do whatever you want!"

So I chose a rich, cranberry red for the second floor music room/ library which was clearly visible from the first floor. The room took five coats of paint, but when we were finished, Harry was thrilled.

Harry was doing his own version of nesting on the outside of the house. He quickly decided he needed to expand the deck and build lighted steps leading from the house down to the dock explaining,

"Now your little toes will never have to touch the ground."

His process was always the same. First, he'd sketch out three different designs, usually on paper napkins. He would then come in and nonchalantly sit down saying,

"I'll show you the choices, and you can decide which one you like best."

He would put the first drawing on the table, and I'd say,

"Hm. That's nice."

He would nod as if I were playing right into his hands and put the second drawing down. Option two was always better, but still somewhat ordinary, and I would say,

"Ah. That's better I think."

He'd nod happily and then slowly, ever so nonchalantly, lay down number three. Option three was always the knock-your-socks-off option, not just imaginative, but wildly ambitious. I would involuntarily clap my hands and gasp,

"Wow! That's amazing! Can you really do that?!" Harry would beam, kiss my hand, and say,

"That's what I'm going for. That little clap. I do it all for you. Do you see?"

So that's how Harry came to single-handedly enlarge the deck with a design like a large gingko leaf,

"Because you do love a leaf."

Once we were permanently settled at the lake, we fell into a fairytale routine. I swear I'm not making this up. Every day, Harry would wake me with a kiss and a cup of coffee. He would then take his own coffee around to the other side and get back into bed. If we happened to have slept in the loft that night, Harry would climb up the ladder and crawl across the floor to my side of the bed, coffee cup held high.

For every thing we did, Harry had a name with "fun" after it. So every morning, we had what Harry termed "morning bed fun" where we would drink our coffee, and I would lie "in the pocket" with my head snuggled on Harry's shoulder, arm across his stomach, and we would talk. Tell stories about our childhoods or stories about our lives before we knew each other, whatever came to mind. Sometimes Harry would make up stories for me. My favorite story, the one I asked him to tell me again and again, was his version of how we would have gotten together if we had known each other in college. This is the story he told me.

When you are walking around campus, every now and then, you get this odd feeling that someone is following you. So you look around quickly, and you see just a flash of movement behind a tree. That's all. So you turn and walk a little further, when suddenly you get that feeling again. You twirl around again and see that same flicker of movement. Because I would be so overwhelmed by your beauty that all I could do was follow you around and love you from afar. But one day, I get my courage up, and I time it just right (because I know your habits) such that you are walking along one way, and I nonchalantly come strolling along the other way, not able to talk to you or even look at you but content just to be close to you. After a couple of months of that, I get my nerve up to walk right by you, and that's when you notice me and see that I am wearing a VERY cool bomber jacket and a hat with something written on it. Then one day, you are sitting on the quad in the spring sunshine, and I look at you, and I see how beautiful you are with the sun on your red hair, and I finally get up the courage to walk right up to you.

So I stand there, dumbstruck, looking at you, and that's when you see what is written on the front of my hat. It's a simple question. "Will you marry me?" If you said, "No," I would turn around and walk away, and on the back of my hat you would see one single word. "Drat." But of course, you wouldn't say, "No." You would say, "Yes," and we would get married and have lots of sex and make lots of babies and live happily ever after. Do you see?"

I see.

Sometimes we talked about the real story of how we got together and about what each of us was thinking and feeling along the way. When I asked Harry whether he believed God put us together, at first he'd say no, but at some point that began to change, and he'd say,

"I don't know. All I know is I married an Irish mystic."

Then we would talk about the day ahead of us, and "morning bed fun" always ended the same way. We'd sing a song Harry taught me from his childhood that his dad sang with them every morning, a song from an old Disney movie about Johnny Appleseed.

Pack your stuff and get a goin'
Get them apple trees a growin'
There's a lot of work out there to do.
Oh there's a lot of work to do.

On the last line, we'd thrust our fists high into the air emphatically and laugh every time.Harry would then go outside to work on whatever project he had underway, declaring,

"It's a bluebird day!"

or looking off into the receding foothills, say,

"There's a five-layer horizon today!"

Harry did not marry me because he wanted a housewife. He never once said to me, "I'm all out of underwear," or, "What's for dinner?" He did his own laundry, scoured out the bathrooms, and if there were no signs of cooking at dinnertime, he put a frozen pizza in the oven. He made me start to believe he married me because he couldn't not marry me. I was just so incredibly beguiling! Every move I made. The first time I decided to make something for dinner, he came into the kitchen and threw his arms in the air, exclaiming,

"And she cooks, too!" and ran to get the camera.

The first batch of cookies I baked sent him running for the camera again, shouting,

"And she bakes, too!"

Everything that ever came out of that oven was documented. He photographed anything cooling on the counter. Every buttermilk raisin scone, every rhubarb pie, every banana muffin, pumpkin tea bread, everything. Sometime during the day, I also always managed to do something he thought was so impossibly charming, he just had to get the camera. One night, I was in bed reading when from the doorway came,

"You're just so cute in your reading glasses!" just before the flash went off.

One of those times was the occasion when Harry christened me with my favorite nickname. He called me by many names, Loveperson, Sconewife, Cellowife, Adventurewife, Lovefaucet, Pumpkinflower, etc. Our prenuptial agreement was that he never had to dance, and I never had to swim. I was deathly afraid of water. Even so, Harry secretly confided to Phaedra that he'd get me swimming, but he never once pushed me about it. While everyone else was urging me to come into the water, Harry was always mum. Playing it cool. One bluebird day, though, after I'd spent another family weekend sitting on the dock dangling my feet in the water while everyone else had "lake fun," I decided it was time to take the plunge. Harry was busy up at the house, so I slipped down to the dock without him seeing. I strapped on a life jacket out of the boat, put two styrofoam "noodles" under me, a third "noodle" around my waist, and slowly inched my way down the ladder into the water. I needn't have worried. I was so buoyant, I was perched on a styrofoam throne barely in the water. I was bobbing a little further out into the cove when I suddenly heard Harry calling,

"Eileenie? Where are you?"

I shouted that I was down at the dock. Harry came tromping through the bushes, took one look at me in the water, threw his arms up in celebration and whooped,

"AQUAWIFE!!"

Suffice it to say there are 12 pictures and a video commemorating my regal ride.

Harry never once complained, kvetched, grumbled, smirked or rolled his eyes. If somehow before he brought me my morning coffee, I had stumbled bleary-eyed out of the bedroom, he threw his arms open wide and greeted me with a huge smile. When I told him my grandmother used to wake me in the morning by calling to me, "Eileen, the morning glories are out," Harry filled the huge planters on the deck with morning glories and twined them up around a trellis. Then he'd wake me in the same way.

Harry was a smart investor, but monthly money tracking made him edgy. I loved household budgeting, but was terrified about investing, so we divided up the money responsibilities and handled talking about it on a need to know basis. One day, before putting an unopened bill on my desk, he scribbled across the top of it in jaunty jubilation,

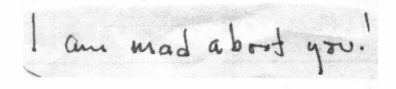

I am mad about you.

Harry also had a very clear role defined for himself as my husband.

"It's my job to take care of you."

A sweet example was the time he saved me from the snake. Even more than water, I feared snakes. Once when Phaedra was five years old, she saw that I was worrying about something and said, "Don't worry, Mommy. The only thing we really have to worry about is snakes, and we don't even live in the woods." Now I was living not only in the woods, but also at a lake. The snakes had squatters rights. It was only a matter of time.

One day shortly after the "Aquawife" episode, Harry decided to fix our neighbors' dock. These neighbors were rarely at the lake, and their dock squeaked day and night with an increasingly loud screech that kept us up at night. Harry finally had enough, so he swam across the cove, a can of WD-40 in a plastic bag clasped between his teeth, to the neighbors' dock and set about oiling every metal surface. I was so cavalier about the water now that I was down to a scant two styrofoam noodles and no life jacket. So I was noodling around in the cove talking with Harry while he worked. Unfortunately, it was spring. Snakes do love the springtime. Suddenly, swimming across my path was a mammoth snake. Since Harry is not here to testify otherwise, you'll just have to take my word for it when I tell you it was a brute. A beast of a snake. I screamed,

"SNAAAAAAAAAAAAAAAKE!!" as loudly as I could.

Hearing my screams, Harry immediately dove into the water. He was a great swimmer, and he got to me in seconds, put himself between me and the snake, splashed a tsunami at the snake, and then swam back to the neighbors' dock, towing me by a noodle. He was absolutely my hero. But then he was faced with the dilemma of getting me back to our own dock across the cove. Harry outlined various options, most of which still involved me getting back into the snake infested water. I was having none of it. So Harry finally decided there was only one thing to do. He swam back across the cove, got in our boat, and motored back to get me. When I got into the boat, Harry said,

"It's such a bluebird day, let's take a little ride."

So off we went. After a lovely look around the lake, Harry took my hand, kissed it, and said,

"I think it's safe to go back. He should be gone by now."

The best part of this story is that, comical as it was, Harry never once laughed at me or chided me for being afraid. He took me the way I was. Took everyone the way they were.

Another time, I had to have surgery on my wrist. The surgeon had not made it clear that I was supposed to start taking the pain pills he prescribed the morning of the surgery, so there would be a good supply in my system. When he heard the mixup, he was quite worried that they wouldn't be able to get the pain under control, and he told Harry I needed a pain pill every hour. When Harry got me back home, we saw how true that was. One pill would get me through just short of an hour before intense pain would start to set in. Not only did Harry tend to me the rest of the day, he set his alarm clock, so that he could wake up every hour on the hour through the night and give me pain pills. All I remember was groggily thinking,

"I'm so crazy about this man," whenever I heard that alarm go off.

After a couple weeks, I was much better, but my right hand was in a cast. I was a little down and complained to Harry about how unkempt my feet looked, so he said,

"I can fix that,"

and set about painting my toenails. He did love to see me in open-toed shoes. Once when we were buying hiking shoes for me, I saw a pair of open-toed, sequined, sling backs that I just had to try on. This was new for me. Something about Harry brought out the female love of shoes in me. When I tried them on, Harry said,

"We're getting those. If all you do is wear them around the house, they'll be worth it!"

One day, before we were even married, I had to contact my former husband about some money situation with Phaedra's schooling. At that time, things between Phaedra's father and me were very strained.

109

I was always visibly anxious about talking with him, and I had been putting off this particular situation as long as I could. Harry asked me what was wrong, and when I told him what I needed to do and how afraid I was, he said calmly,

"I'll handle it. You can stand behind me."

Harry did much more than simply "handle it." He regularly communicated with my daughters' father with calm, cordial e-mails, sharing news and tactfully tackling money matters. Harry's diplomacy and intercession started the healing between my former husband and me that still bears fruit today. I was bowled over. It wasn't just the relief of Harry taking this task off my shoulders. Harry was my safe place. I could run to him and crying,

"Sanctuary!"

and I'd be safe. Harry would protect me. No one in my life had ever wanted to protect me before.

I am not a talkative person, but I found that I just babbled away to him, especially when we were riding in the Highlander, now known to us as The Green Bubble. I surprised even myself, and frequently apologized,

"I'm sorry. I'm babbling." But he would always say,

"Don't say that. I need to know everything that's going on in your head. It's important."

Every night, we would lie in bed, me "in the pocket," and Harry would read to me. He would read the wonderful fishing stories of John Gierach or the poems of Billy Collins, but he especially loved the poet Ted Kooser. Harry had heard a radio interview with Kooser and became intrigued, so he went out and bought Kooser's collection Flying at Night. He loved Kooser's midwestern voice and imagery, and

110

he gave me the Kooser collections Sure Signs, Local Wonders, and Delights & Shadows the next couple Christmases. He loved Flying at Night the most, though, and this was one of his favorite Kooser poems which he read to me often.

A Widow

She's combed his neckties out of her hair
and torn out the tongues of his shoes.
She's poured his ashes out of their urn
and into his humidor. For the very last time,
she's scrubbed the floor around the toilet.
She hates him even more for dying.

He would read it to me and say,

"Do you see? She misses everything about him. Even the things that used to annoy her."

Once, seeing my somewhat concerned reaction to this, he lightened the mood by smiling and promising,

"If I die first, I'll come back and flush all the toilets, so you'll know it's me."

Harry taught me how to let things go, and he showed me the healing power of forgiveness. If I said or did something I regretted, and I told him I was sorry, he always said without fail,

"Don't worry. I forgave you as soon as you said it."

Harry made me feel like the queen of the world. Everyday we were together, he told me,

"You're so beautiful."

I was 57 years old! But he made me feel like he didn't just love me, he adored me. I felt sorry for all the other women in the world because none of them were married to Harry. His love enfolded me, so that even when he wasn't around, I glowed with its warmth. After living my entire life feeling always on the outside, Harry brought me inside. Brought me home.

Do you see?

Harry at the lake.

"Nobody here loves me!"
- Harry

~ Dress Rehearsal ~

God loves symmetry. Darkness followed by light. Before grown into after. This is Harry's and my "before". Before God had our full attention.

For several years, Harry had been contending with increasingly debilitating pain in his right knee. He had done a couple rounds of the "chicken shots" and had arthroscopic surgery, but neither gave him lasting relief. Harry loved the outdoors and wanted to be able to hike the many mountain trails at the lake, so he finally decided to look into knee replacement surgery. Through his work at the University of North Carolina, Harry had become friends with Dr. Thomas Fehring, a highly respected orthopedist. Harry knew Tom's excellent reputation and had complete confidence in him, so we went up to Charlotte for Tom to take a look at Harry's knee. Tom confirmed that Harry's knee function was essentially bone-on-bone, and we decided it was best for Harry to have the knee replacement surgery in early 2005.

In February, 2005, we drove back up to Charlotte for the surgery. The plan was for me to sleep at Harry's brother Larry's home for the few days that Harry would be in Charlotte's excellent Presbyterian Orthopedic Hospital. We were not anticipating any problems, and as we sat in the parking lot while Harry smoked one last cigar, we were blithely oblivious to the gathering storm.

The surgery went well, and we spent the first day with Harry sleeping off the anesthetic and me reading in a chair by his bed. At about seven that evening, I kissed Harry good-bye and drove back to Larry and Donna's. I went to bed and slept soundly. All was calm, all was bright. This was going to be a piece of cake.

The next morning, I confidently drove back to the hospital, cheerily chatted with the cafeteria cashier while I paid for two coffees, and took the elevator up to the third floor. When I got off the elevator, I was alarmed to hear Harry's voice from way down the hall. I couldn't make out what he was saying, but it didn't sound good. As I got closer to Harry's room, I could hear that he was arguing with someone. When I got into the room, I saw a nurse calmly trying to cajole Harry into swinging his legs over the side of the bed. I knew this was Harry only because this was his room, and the patient in the bed looked exactly like Harry, but this was not my loveperson. This was someone I'd never met. He was screaming in pain and shouting at her to let him alone in no uncertain terms. As soon as he saw me, he shouted,

"Tell her to leave me alone!"

Only later did I figure out what was going on. I realized that not only was Harry in pain, he was also battling through his first day without nicotine. Have you ever tried to quit smoking or lived with anyone who was trying to quit? I never had before. Harry subsequently tried to quit smoking many times, and he began each attempt by telling me,

"Keep your distance. There's nothing you can do to help, and I'm sorry ahead of time for anything I say. I love you, and I don't mean any of it."

114

But I didn't know any of this yet, so the person in Harry's room was a stranger to me, more so as the day progressed. Harry snapped at everyone who came in, the nurses, the orderlies, the therapists. Everyone except Tom Fehring. Everyday, when Tom came into the room, Harry became the soul of stouthearted affability, upbeat and joking until Tom left.

I was completely flummoxed. Kisses and sweet nothings didn't dent his dour mood. My attempts at consolation actually seemed to make things worse. I zigzagged through the mine fields of that day making one misstep after another before I finally left for the evening exhausted and bewildered.

The next day was no better. Harry continued to be angry and recalcitrant. He screamed in pain when they tried to get him out of bed, and he refused to go to physical therapy. He complained about everything. The bed, the pillows, the food, the temperature, the sun coming in the windows, everything he beheld. At one point, he tore the hospital ID band off his wrist and threw it across the room.

Never having experienced knee surgery myself, I had no idea how to assess what was happening with Harry. I did notice that in the group physical therapy sessions, several patients who were older than Harry seemed to be doing considerably better. They did the exercises and managed to be civil, but Harry sat in his wheelchair refusing to participate and complaining about the pain. When I passed the nurses' station, they always stopped talking, watched me walk by, then started whispering again when they thought I was out of earshot. Harry had insulted every one of them at one time or another, and I felt like a peace offering was in order. One morning before I got to the hospital, I drove to a Godiva store at a mall and bought a ten pound box of truffles. When I got to the hospital, before going to Harry's room, I went to the nurses' station. Luckily, they were all there. I put the box of truffles on the countertop and said with all sincerity,

115

"I really appreciate how patient you've been with my husband. I'm so sorry for the way he's been acting," silently begging them not to wreak some sort of revenge on him.

They nodded silently, but looked warily at the candy as if chocolate couldn't come close to fixing this.

"This really is not like him at all," I continued as abjectly as I could.

More noncommittal nodding.

"This pain he's having," I asked, perplexed, "is this normal? Is it really that bad?"

They gave each other knowing glances, and then all looked at me.

"No," they tersely chorused.

They did not smile when I left.

That afternoon I went down to the cafeteria to try to find something, anything, Harry might eat. I loaded up a tray with several possibilities and took it back up to his room. By that point, the nurses had managed to get Harry out of the bed and into a chair. Just as I got in the door, Harry's cellphone rang across the room over by the bed. I went over and got it, saw that it was Harry's daughter-in-law, Emily, and handed the phone to Harry. As I finished setting all the food out on his hospital bed tray, I heard Harry tell Emily in a whining wail,

"Nobody here loves me!"

I was shocked, appalled, and angered all at the same time. My goodwill was gone. I was keenly aware of John's reservations about our marrying, and I was humiliated to think that now John would think he'd been right all along. I asked Harry for the phone, wanting to try to do some damage control, but when I said, "Hi," the person on the other end who answered was not Emily. It was Harry's son, John.

"What's going on over there?! Why is Pop saying nobody loves him?!" John asked accusingly.

Everything I said in reply sounded like an excuse. I was mortified.

That was the low point. Things did not improve. Harry and I could not have been further apart. My patience was gone, and my attention was turned to my own embarrassment. Pride ran roughshod over each of us with predictable results. "We" split into "me."

The day Harry was to leave the hospital, I folded down the back seats of Harry's Highlander and made a pallet of camping mattresses, blankets, and pillows, so Harry could stretch out and sleep. Larry and Donna came to the hospital to see us off, but we were so clearly irritated with each other that Larry joked about whether I wanted to take Harry back home with me at all. I wondered that myself. I got Harry settled, got in the driver's seat, and headed out on the three hour trip back to the lake wondering what was next.

But God let all that bide.

Our hour had not yet come.

"I just want my brothers to see how much we love each other."
- Harry

~ The Trip of a Lifetime ~

There's an old saying. "If you want to make God laugh, tell Him your plans." When Harry and I got married, our plan was to travel the world together. There were still several rivers in the West where Harry wanted to fly fish, and he had never seen the Grand Canyon. I had never been to Paris, and we both wanted to go to Ireland and see where our ancestors had lived. But here we were in the summer of 2006, two years into our life together, and all our traveling so far had been us driving thither and yon in The Green Bubble on "The Harry and Eileen Roadshow". We each wanted the other to be comfortably nestled into our respective families, but we felt like we were accomplishing that at warp speed. We were barely married before we were off to a reunion of my family at the North Carolina coast. Two weeks later, we hosted a reunion of Harry's brothers at our lake house. Wanting to make a good impression, I was a whirling dervish, matching these towels with that shower curtain, switching this shade to that lamp, swapping this picture for the one over there, trying to make everything "perfect," but Harry finally sat me down, took my hands, kissed my forehead, and said,

"Stop now. None of this matters. I just want my brothers to see how much we love each other."

That much we managed to accomplish. From then on there were trips out to visit my daughter, Jessamin, in Phoenix, Arizona, my Aunt Eileen in Los Banos, California, and Harry's brothers in Ventura and Novato, California. When The Roadshow wasn't on the road, our home was a revolving door of visiting family, Harry's brother, Don, once happily chirping, "This place is like a resort!," as I offered him a couple of just-out-of-the-dryer beach towels to take with him on his way out to the lake. We'd also made several emergency trips to help various siblings or children out of some difficulty. In addition, after the birth of John and Emily's son, Finn, Harry and I made the 13-hour drive to New Jersey several times a year. All this to shore up and support our families. All this to fulfill the mission Harry recognized for us to, "...let all this love overflow onto everyone else we love and help make their lives better."

We finally came to a point, however, where we longed for some of that promised traveling by ourselves. We felt we had done good work, and work it had been. Now we wanted an adventure together. We wanted something completely different. We wanted to go somewhere neither of us had ever been. Somewhere new that was completely ours. We thought Italy was that place.

God had a completely different place in mind.

The Alumni Association at the University of Iowa had regularly been sending us brochures of various tours they sponsored, and in early 2006, we got a brochure about a trip to Italy starting October 9, 2006. Seven nights and eight days leisurely touring Venice, Florence, and Rome. Neither of us had ever been to Italy, but my father had served there in World War II and always wanted to go back. Harry had lived in Europe, but never managed to get to Italy and had always regretted that. As for myself, I wanted to explore our Catholic roots in Rome. So we sent in our deposit, and Harry set about planning a couple extra days in Rome. He was delighted and started playing

119

Italian language tapes, so we could learn enough of the language to get by. Languages came easily to Harry, and I relied on him to figure out how to get us around Rome, but he seemed mainly interested in learning how to say "my beautiful cello wife" in Italian, and would call to me from his office,

"Mia bellezza!"

The spring and summer of 2006 flew by in the usual frenzied way. At the end of July, Harry's brothers all came for their yearly reunion to the lake. In August, John, Emily, Jennifer, and Finn came for a week with Jill and Phaedra coming for a couple days each as well. All our visitors endlessly advised us on where we should go, what we should be sure to see, what kinds of clothes we should pack, what we should eat, etc. Through all of it, Harry seemed his usual, good natured self, joking in an exaggerated Italian accent.

Harry also embarked on another project. He had always admired the hand-stacked rock walls in New England and wanted to build one himself. Now inspired by all things Italian, he designed an ambitious "water feature," an Italian style pergola with decking surrounded by a river rock wall. In September, he borrowed a friend's backhoe and excavated a large area down at the edge of the lake. He then ordered several tons of river rock, but our lot was just wooded enough so that when the truck came to deliver the rocks, it couldn't get farther into our yard than the edge of the driveway. The rocks were unceremoniously dumped beside the house in a pile. In between the various visits we were hosting, Harry started moving the rock pile, one wheelbarrow at a time, closer to the excavation site. That's what he had been doing right before our good friends Stu and Suzy French came to visit. We had a wonderful time taking boat rides at dusk, playing cards, and talking about the wonders we would experience in Italy.

On Friday, September 29, we waved good-bye to Stu and Suzy, and

Harry went out to the rock pile to move some rocks before Larry and Donna arrived early that evening. It wasn't long, however, before he came back in the house feeling tired and a little woozy. He tried to lie down, but started throwing up. We were both a little alarmed, but we thought it must have been something he'd eaten. He continued to feel badly through the rest of the day, and by the time Larry and Donna arrived, he could not even get out of bed. They understandingly left Saturday morning, and I tried to make Harry as comfortable as possible. Nothing seemed to help. He called our friend and neighbor, Bill Plummer, who was also his internist. He and Bill discussed several possibilities, ultimately deciding to watch and wait. At that point, I was convinced Harry had picked up some kind of bacterial infection in the lake, and after a little rest, he seemed somewhat better.

However, by the end of the next week, Harry was clearly getting worse. On October 6, the Friday right before we were supposed to fly to Italy, Bill told Harry to go to the hospital in the little town of Seneca for some tests. Harry laid in the back seat of The Green Bubble while I drove the 30 minutes to Oconee Memorial Hospital. Bill was there waiting for us, and he immediately got Harry in for a CAT scan and blood work. Bill rushed the tests through, and by noon, he concluded that Harry was anemic, and he ordered three units of blood. Getting this all arranged took some doing, and it wasn't until late in the afternoon that they were able to start the transfusion. In the meantime, Bill assured me that, even though they had to send the blood work off for analysis, he had looked at the blood samples himself and nothing looked alarming. I felt better.

The day after the transfusion, Harry felt stronger, and we weighed the pros and cons of going to Italy. He did not want to be the cause of our missing out on our trip, but I assured him that Italy was always going to be there, and I voted for staying put until we had an answer for what was making him ill. That afternoon, Harry e-mailed our family and friends the following:

121

We are not going to Italy. This we decided today at around 11:00 a.m. Here is why.

We hosted Stu and Suzy French here at the lake on the 27th and 28th of September and had a grand time. We finished their visit on Thursday night with a great steak dinner at which I ate gluttonously. On Friday morning, I experienced diarrhea and vomiting and thought it was probably caused by something that I ate. Perhaps it was. Anyhow, we bade Stu and Suzy goodbye and prepared for the arrival of Larry and Donna, with whom we were to tour the mountains in search of retirement location candidates for their eventual retirement. They arrived at 7:00 p.m.. I threw up again at 6:50 p.m. and looked quite sick when they arrived. I insisted that I was and would be ok, but I was wrong. Larry and Donna graciously returned to Charlotte on Saturday while I laid around and spoke to my doc by phone. He thought that I might have an ulcer caused by the ibuprofen that I take for arthritis, so I stopped drinking coffee and eating anything that tasted good, like chocolate and ice cream. On Sunday, I threw up again but generally began to feel better. We spent Monday and Tuesday doing chores in anticipation of our trip to Italy, and I remained relatively weak and without appetite. By Wednesday, the weakness was worse and by Thursday was really profound. I could not go up the stairs without resting at the top.

Yesterday I went to see the doc, who ordered lots of blood work, chest x-ray, and CAT scan of the stomach area. By noon, the results were back and confirmed his suspicion that I was suffering from anemia. He ordered 3 units of blood, and Eileen and I had a lovely time in the hospital till 1:00 a.m. getting this blood from the little baggies into me. My weakness disappeared entirely, and I now feel fine, but a little tired from the long day.

As we were scheduled to leave for the Atlanta airport at 10:00 a.m. tomorrow, we had to decide whether to go to Italy or not. We decided ultimately that the risk/reward ratio was too high and will stay home. More lab tests are due this coming week and will probably confirm my doc's hypothesis that this is some kind of "viral syndrome". He is having weird stuff like Lyme

disease checked as well. It is likely that we will never know for sure what hit
me, but if we do, I'll let you all know. For now, we know that all of the read-
ily recognizable things can be ruled out, and this includes all of the really
scary stuff like silent heart attack, emphysema, and so on. My blood "looks"
like a viral syndrome is the answer. Some little bodies therein are segmented
rather than round as is normal.

Eileen and I are both very glad that we did not encounter this difficulty in
Italy, and we want to stay put until all of this is resolved. I plan to spend my
"Italy time" working in the yard.

Love to you all,
Harry

We spent the weekend mainly sitting by a fire letting Harry rest,
counting our blessings that this had happened while we were still
home instead of in another country, and telling each other everything
would be all right. Harry felt better, so it seemed there was every reason to feel reassured that this was just some passing problem. After
all, hadn't he just been lugging rocks around the yard?

I tried to remember what Bill had said, and I tried not to worry, but
my nerves kept crackling with a prickly charge as a distant siren
sounded in the recesses of my mind.

Why would a healthy person suddenly need three units of blood?

"Somebody has to be in that 10 percent. Why not me?"
- Harry

~ Diagnosis ~

"It's leukemia."

Harry sat at the end of the dining room table still holding the phone in his hand. Gravity suddenly failed, and the earth went spinning off without us. Neither of us said a word. We couldn't. The breath was knocked out of us. All I could think was, "I will not fall apart. I will not fall apart."

"Bill says we have to get to Saint Francis hospital right away. He was crying."

All I could do was nod. Like robots, we both got up from the table, got our coats, and headed to the car. We were supposed to be on a plane to Italy. We were supposed to finally be taking that trip we'd dreamed of when we got married. All those trips to see family, to re-unions, to kids. We were supposed to finally be taking a trip just for us. Now we were racing to Saint Francis hospital in Greenville, South Carolina, terrified that Harry had only hours to live. I called our priest, Father Thomas Miles, from the car. Crying, I left him a message begging him to meet us at the hospital. When nearly an hour later we

124

finally arrived and were circling the parking lot, Dr. Mark O'Rourke, the oncologist Bill had hurriedly brought in, called on Harry's cell phone,

"Where are you?!!"

"We're trying to find a place to park."

"Go to valet parking!! Get in here!!"

When we finally got into the hospital, a nurse met us in the lobby and took us directly up to the fifth floor where Dr. O'Rourke and his partners have a special unit for their leukemia patients. Once on the fifth floor, the nurse took us to a vacant hospital room where we both sat stiffly on the edge of the bed. Dr. O'Rourke just had a moment to talk to us, but he said he'd be back later as they were hoping to start treatment that very day.

Shortly after O'Rourke left Father Miles walked into the room. He had gotten my message and hurriedly left the meeting he was in to come to us. We both choked up at the sight of him, and Harry asked Father to hear his confession. The two of them went next door to a little chapel while I waited in a daze. There were no thoughts in my head. My mind had completely shut down. After awhile, Father Miles came back to where I was and sat down on the bed next to me. He didn't say a word. I asked him where Harry was, and he said Harry was still in the chapel praying. That's when I finally broke down, collapsing into our dear priest's arms. Father Miles just held me until I finally stopped sobbing.

After Father Miles left, a very kind nurse helped us get settled. The first thing we were astonished to discover was that there was a crucifix hanging in every room. We were amazed and grateful to have been led to an actual Catholic hospital in the South. The nurse started to explain what we could expect. She told us that the treatment would take at least a month. At this, Harry gasped audibly and exclaimed,

"You mean I'll be alive for at least another month?!"

We were giddy at this good news. We had thought he might be dead by the end of the day. We both started laughing with relief. The nurse was surprised at how well we were taking what she thought was bad news. She further amazed us by asking whether Harry wanted to receive the Eucharist every day. We just looked at each other. Harry said yes he would, and she told us she would make a note in his chart. We were stunned.

What kind of place had God brought us to?

We spent the rest of the day doing paperwork and reading their many pamphlets on leukemia. Dr. O'Rourke finally returned early that evening. He had a Jersey Mike's tuna sub with him for us. Harry and I had not had anything to eat yet that day, and one of the nurses had called O'Rourke and told him to pick up a sub for us on the way back to the hospital.

O'Rourke explained that he believed Harry had acute myelogenous leukemia (AML). He said it was bad, but not the worst. He told us that 10 percent of patients survived this form of leukemia. At this, we were absolutely jubilant. It was possible to survive this thing?! Harry and I just looked at each other with wide, megagrins. O'Rourke was confused, so Harry explained,

"Someone has to be in that 10 percent. Why not me?"

At that point, we didn't even care what O'Rourke had to say next. We had hope. Genuine, statistically validated hope.

O'Rourke explained that he wanted to put Harry on an experimental program. He had hoped to start that day, but the protocol required a baseline bone marrow biopsy before they could start treatment. They were going to do the biopsy the next day, expedite the results, and hopefully get the chemotherapy started the same day. Having gotten all the medical information out of the way, O'Rourke said Bill told him we were supposed to be on a plane to Italy right that moment. He told us that he himself had just come back from a two week trip to Italy during which he attended one of the weekly Wednesday audiences with Pope Benedict. Now we were really agog. We were in a Catholic hospital with a Catholic doctor where they'd made a note in Harry's medical chart that he wanted to receive the Eucharist every day. More astoundingly, before he left, O'Rourke prayed with us, a practice we maintained nearly every day to come.

Someone was clearly in charge. Someone had a plan.

But I was afraid to trust God's plan because I was afraid it was going to hurt too much. Pope John Paul II used to say that the future frightened us because whatever we were imagining hadn't happened yet, so God hadn't yet given us the grace to cope with it. That's exactly where I was.

After O'Rourke left, Harry and I went down to sit in our Green Bubble together while Harry smoked his last cigar. We got in the car, and for the first time that day, we clung to each other and cried. I felt that maddening helplessness that no matter how hard you held onto someone, you couldn't reach through that invisible barrier - that impermeable space between the one who's going and the one who's left behind - and pull them back over to where you are. Harry held me tightly and cried,

"I'm not afraid for me. I'm just so scared for you."

Harry, filled with self-pity during our dry run, now had tears only for me. When there was no more to say, nowhere to go, we went back into our new home. The nurse tried to get us to eat some of the sub, but neither of us could get down a bite. We laid on the bed together for awhile, and then the nurse came in and gave Harry something to help him sleep. I made a bed on the recliner next to his bed and lay down to try to rest. The kind nurse actually came and tucked a blanket around me, kissed my forehead, and said good night.

We were not in Italy.

We were in another world entirely.

"There are miles and miles of skyward hope above."
- Harry

~ Nesting at Saint Francis ~

Harry decided to stay at Saint Francis in Greenville rather than go anywhere else for treatment. We couldn't believe God had landed us in such a wonderful place. It meant a lot to Harry that Saint Francis was a Catholic hospital, that he could receive the Eucharist everyday, that there was a tabernacle right downstairs, and that they even celebrated Mass every Wednesday. Harry's son, John, tried to talk him into going to New York City, but Harry's thought, verified by O'Rourke, was that the protocol was the same no matter what hospital he was in, so he wanted to be where he was comfortable, and we both had family and friends for support. Besides, Harry trusted Bill Plummer, and Bill had brought in Mark O'Rourke, so Harry had complete trust in O'Rourke as well. He was also very impressed with the nurses and comforted that both they and O'Rourke prayed with us throughout the day. Most of all, it was very important to him to know the lake house was just 45 minutes away. He hung onto the hope that he might actually live to go back there someday soon.

As for me, I had no control over anything, but I could at least build us a nest at Saint Francis. There was no chance I was going to leave Harry's side and sleep at the lake, so I set about bringing home to Saint Francis. First, I bought a twin size Aerobed® for me to sleep on that fit perfectly in the niche under the window in Harry's hospital room, close enough for us to hold hands. From home, I brought a quilt Donna had made for Harry as well as the comforter off our bed, each of our bedside lamps, colorful sheets, and Harry's favorite pillow. There was a washer and dryer on the top floor of the hospital, and my plan was to wash and change the sheets every day, so Harry would have that added touch of home. The nurses looked concerned and explained that I could only keep doing the sheets until Harry's white count dropped to a certain level. When that happened, he would need to sleep on only the sterilized linens the hospital provided, but I was determined to keep washing the sheets from home until we reached that point. I also brought two 4'x5' collages of family pictures that we had made, and I put those up in the room. I brought books, CDs, "The Great Courses" audio tapes, my flute, and, most importantly, our wedding picture. Harry was greatly cheered.

Harry lying on my Aerobed® at Saint Francis. The bag over his shoulder is the chemotherapy pump.

Harry next to his bed at Saint Francis with a reading lamp, comforter, photo collage, audio tapes, and a statue of the Blessed Mother.

When my daughter Phaedra came down from East Tennessee State University, she set up a blog for us, so we could let our family and friends know what was going on, and "The Daily Leamy Blog" was launched. For several days, she took up the gauntlet and wrote the blog entries for us.

The Daily Leamy Blog - Saturday, October 14, 2006

Today was a good day. This was day 3 of chemo, and there are still no side effects. So far the chemo treatment has been delightfully uneventful. Harry and Eileen took their morning walk around the hospital. After getting settled back into the hospital room, the usual round of nurses and doctors made a steady flow in and out of the room, checking Harry's vital signs and things of that nature. Visitors and nurses are outfitted with gowns and masks, so as not to bring outside germs into the room. Phaedra came to visit around 11 a.m. and joined them for an afternoon two mile walk. Harry, ever true to his boy scout roots, pointed out the various kinds of trees and plants along the hospital trail. It was "bluebird" weather, as Harry likes to say.

Harry is quite confident and comfortable in his little cocoon there at St. Francis Hospital with Eileen by his side. He keeps himself busy with books, lecture tapes, and Bach. Those who know Harry never doubt his strength (physical and mental) or optimism. We know that both of these things will see him through this. Of course he also has the support, love, and positivity of his family and friends.

Tomorrow Harry begins the fourth day of chemo. He will be given two new medications, Daunorubicin and Cytarabine, which will continue for 7 days. There will be more details about medications and procedures tomorrow, as well as some helpful links and information. For now we wanted to keep the daily report from St. Francis short and sweet.

The Daily Leamy Blog - Sunday, October 15, 2006

Day 4 is in the books! The Daunorubicin and the Cytarabine are working quietly in Harry's system with no negative side effects. However, because of these new drugs, Harry must remain attached to the medication pump and is unable to take his daily walks outside. He is still able to walk through the hallways though, just so long as he stays connected to the medication pump and wears his mask.

Eileen continues to tend to Harry carefully and lovingly. It is, of course, a great comfort for Harry to have Eileen by his side through the day and night. Their fervent love is truly a presence in the room.

John and Jennifer brought love and laughter from New York as they sat at Harry's bedside today. They will stay through Monday.

There was a lively conversation today about Hostess cupcakes. Harry, as it turns out, can discuss these and similar chocolatey items at length. Deep down though, Harry believes them all to be lesser versions of his beloved chocolate cream pie. In fact, he has a chocolate creme pie sitting in the hospital fridge - a present from his doctor. After a good night chat with Finn, Harry beds down each night with a Montana travel guide. He cannot wait to get back into his waders. Harry and Eileen remain strong and optimistic. They greet the sun each morning with a smile.

It is important to reiterate that Harry has been diagnosed with AML, subtype M2 (with maturation). He had previously written that he was diagnosed with M1; this was a typo. They are treated the same way.

More about the two drugs he received today:

Daunorubicin is an anti-tumor antibiotic, also called an anthracyline antibiotic. It interacts directly with the DNA in the nucleus of cells interfering with cell survival. Cytarabine is an antimetabolite. This is a chemical that is very similar to the natural building blocks of DNA or RNA, but it exchanges sufficiently from the natural chemical. This drug will substitute for it and block the cell's ability to form DNA or RNA as to prevent the cell from growing. This combination of drugs is a highly common form of inductive chemotherapy for leukemia. Basically, they will act in different ways to prevent DNA synthesis of leukemia cells, stopping their growth and killing them off. The goal of these two drugs is to rid the bone marrow of visible leukemic blast cells. For the chemotherapy to be effective the blood cells will essentially be eliminated from the marrow. This round of chemotherapy will last for 10 days.

(See Harry's note today below)

Additional chemo drugs were added today to the ongoing Genasense drip, and so far, no ill effects.

John and Jen came down from New York for a visit, which was delightful and still is. They leave tomorrow afternoon, so we will have still more time to visit.

The work around me is picking up in intensity while I lie still and feel awkward about it. Sheets now changed daily, masks and gowns, lots of cleaning. All visitors are admonished not to touch my urine - it is apparently toxic. But I am smiling. There are miles and miles of skyward hope above.

After Phaedra went back to school, Harry took over writing the blog himself and happily wrote:

The Daily Leamy Blog - Monday, October 16, 2006

Today was a very excellent day. John, Jen, and Phaedra were here most of the time, and we had plenty of laughs as well as a communal hike of one mile in duration around the perimeter of the 5th floor of the hospital. As it happens, it takes 13 circuits to make a mile, and by the time we had finished, we had attracted attention from the whole population. This particularly as some of our masks were decorated a la "Planet of the Apes".

I remain free of nausea and find only that my appetite is diminishing, which is normal. In other words, I don't feel sick.

The licensure police here at the hospital asked that we take out our bedside lamps for reasons of tripping and fire hazard, and we did. We now have LED

134

headlights for reading in bed and playing light saber. The nurses have mounted a campaign to get us our lamps back, and we will see.

Harry

The Daily Leamy Blog - Tuesday, October 16, 2006

First, my appreciation to all of you who have taken to the blog rather than using email. It helps keep the volume of email down and, even so, I could not answer them all. Not that I am sick and weak. I am not. Today was another good day. We walked a mile within the hospital, I got new chemo drug refills, and got in some good reading and sleeping.

Eileen and Phaedra went out to the store and returned with three Coleman camping lamps. These are made to look like the old gas lanterns, but use batteries instead. So our room has taken on a sort of "camping" theme.

The road ahead consists of 4 more days of chemo followed by 7 days of rest, followed by a bone marrow biopsy test to see if remission was induced. If so, I go home for a bit more rest before returning for the "consolidation" chemo treatments. Stay tuned.

I am buoyed up by the many kind expressions of support from everyone, but most especially from Eileen, who is literally living here in the hospital with me and is protecting me from myself and from those who would distract me from my job, which is to stay healthy and rested through the chemo and beyond. She is a gift from God.

Love,
Harry

The Daily Leamy Blog - Wednesday, October 18, 2006

Another day of loafing, reading, and listening to lectures on tape. No bad reaction to the chemo other than general lassitude. I did make a mile hike around the 5th floor with Larry and daughter Jill in tow, Eileen leading the way. I enjoyed it, and it was great to talk to them without doing so from a bed. We had a nice visit.

Today, we were to have been in Rome. Drat. In fact, we do not a bit regret the decision to stay here. I cannot imagine what it would be like to be doing this in Italy, but it could not be better than here, cappuccino notwithstanding.

I also received a visit from the president of our parish's Knights of Columbus council, who expressed supportive sentiments from the whole group.

These visits, the ongoing chemo, and just the general rhythm of hospital routines make me tired. I am told that this is right on schedule.

Ok, a lecture tidbit: "pyrrhic victory" is one which comes at high cost. It is named for a 4th century (BC) Macedonian general who was hired by the Greeks in southern Italy to take on the Romans. He won, but declared that another such victory would be the end of his army. Good, eh?

A final note of positive effect. I have three spots on my forehead that I know, by experience now, are going to become full blown basal cell carcinomas. These we fair skinned people refer to simply as BCCs. I get a couple removed each year. Well, these three are shrinking, and my doc says that, yes, he could put the dermatologists out of business with this chemo regimen if people would just let him do it.

Love to you all,
Harry

The Daily Leamy Blog - Thursday, October 19, 2006

Two more days to go! Still no nausea, appetite ok, etc. My blood counts are falling rapidly now, and I am feeling it. I seem unable to focus my thoughts on much of anything and information that does enter the noggin seems to flow through without much impact. Maybe this is not new. Anyhow, I feel floaty. The nurses say that this is entirely normal and expected, but I feel dopey. Tomorrow, I will be more so, and may ask Eileen to post the daily update. Again, I feel fine, just disconnected.

We got our lamps back! Eileen decided to speak with someone other than a floor nurse and so went down to the administrative section of the hospital and found the most imposing looking woman in the area. Eileenie told her of our lamps, our loss of them, and the joy that bringing them back would afford. We had them back in no time, with just a perfunctory check of the cords to see whether they were frayed. They were not. The room now is more, much more, like home and we are comfortable and happy in it.

Eileen wants to add one thing. Here it is. -----

Today the Eucharistic minister who came described what we are going through as "going on retreat". We have been physically taken away from the lovely distractions of our previous life and now have been given the opportunity to focus on God and His plan. This we are taking seriously and gratefully. Finally, our thanks to all of you for your support. Your cards and letters are most joyously received.

The Daily Leamy Blog - Friday, October 20, 2006

Eileen is typing this post for me because I find myself rather fatigued. That said, my spirits are good, my appetite remains good, and I am very aware of the wonderful support that I am receiving from Eileen and all of you.

The doctor tells me that after this round of chemo is completed, it will take another 10-12 days before I start to recover from the treatment. That is a time that I'm really looking forward to.

In spite of my fatigue, today I set a new personal best - trumpets please - 17

LAPS around the unit (a mile is 13 laps). Eileen keeps telling me we need to put these daily triumphs on a spreadsheet. We do love a spreadsheet.

The Daily Leamy Blog - Saturday, October 21, 2006

Harry is doing just astoundingly. Though he had a bad night, his spirits are very good, and that 13 laps was a real victory. He's quite weak and tired, but only in body.

I've been thinking about something I'd like to share with all of you. There is holy work and a great gift in this for all of us. Let me explain. I've been thinking about all the many healings Jesus did - how this person would say, "Just let me touch your cloak," or that person would say, "Only say the word... ." But there's one story in Mark, Chapter 2 about the healing of the paralytic. We never hear a word from the paralytic himself - Mark only talks about the actions of his friends. Jesus had come back to Capernaum and word got around that he was at home. Throngs gathered many people deep, and Jesus preached to them. One group came to Him carrying their friend, a paralytic. "Unable to get near Jesus because of the crowd, they opened up the roof above him. After they had broken through, they let down the mat on which the paralytic was lying. When Jesus saw their faith, He said to the paralytic, 'I say to you, rise, pick up your mat, and go home.' He rose, picked up his mat at once, and went away in the sight of everyone. They were all astounded and glorified God, saying, 'We have never seen anything like this.'" Now these were some true friends. They must have been at this fellow's house talking and saying, "You know, if we could just get him to this Jesus guy, he'd be cured for sure." So they carried him who knows how long or how far, only to be confronted by the throng too deep to wade through. But their faith and determination was so strong, they carried the man right up to the top of the house and tore the roof off the place to lower him down to Jesus. Just tore the roof right off. Can you imagine what it must have been like for them when they saw their friend pick up that mat and walk out? They must have rolled back down, lain on the ground exhausted, panting and sweaty, but looked at each other with a smile that said, "We did it. God did it." What a great, great reward and blessing that was for them as well as him. To have been the instrument of his healing was an act of holiness.

I think God loves that kind of brazen faith - that no-holds-barred, nothing's going to stop me faith. So here's what I say. I say we each put a hand under this hospital bed, climb right up through the clouds and tear the roof off Heaven.

I love you all.
Eileen

The Daily Leamy Blog - Saturday, October 21, 2006

Eileenie is typing for me. First, a clarification on the word "day." This is "day" 10. A day on the chemo ward begins when a chemo bag is hung on the IV tree. A "day" runs from the time the chemo is hung until noon the next day. This means that at noon tomorrow, chemo infusion will be over. I am looking forward to it.

This morning I was visited by nausea, diarrhea and dehydration, all par for the course. They knocked me flat, but with the help of rehydration via IV, I am now beginning to feel more nearly normal. I find myself wondering how people coped before the advent of plastic bags, tubing, fittings, syringes and the like. We use a lot of these items in this room. (Note from Eileen - Harry STILL walked 13 laps today, astounding me, the nurses, and himself.)

Till tomorrow...

The Daily Leamy Blog - Sunday, October 22, 2006
(Eileen typing)

The chemo bags are gone, and I am happy about that. The effects of the chemo, even though the bags are gone, continue to escalate, so that this morning, I didn't make my usual walk. As of this writing, I feel much better than I did this morning, and I intend to get up tomorrow morning and kick the bottom out of this thing.

I think of you all often, but phone calls are very wearing, so I'm asking Eileen to turn off the phone for awhile. I will continue to dictate a daily blog as best I can.

(Note from Eileen - Today was a "normal" but very tough day. Harry spiked a fever which is normal when platelets drop. At one point, they gave him some morphine, and his mood, during the brief time he was awake, was GREATLY improved. That doesn't seem fair, now, does it? I had to rely on a couple Hershey's Kisses. No comparison.)

Till tomorrow...

The Daily Leamy Blog - Monday, October 23, 2006
(Eileen typing)

I feel better. After having eaten nothing yesterday and walked not at all, I regained an appetite for both today.

As it happens, my blood is infected with a gram positive bacteria of some kind, and they are treating it with an antibiotic IV drip. (Note from E. - they tell us infection is expected - "part of the game when you play with chemo").

So, today I walked - DRUM ROLL PLEASE - TWO MILES. (From E - we now refer to laps over 13 as GLs - "gravy laps"). I also felt focused enough to do some reading and ate most of my food. (From E. - I'm catching on to bring him a chocolate dessert from the cafeteria - works like a charm.).

A very sweet nun from St. Anthony's School came by with the Holy Eucharist for both of us, and that gave the day a considerably brighter start.

One final note on the topic of Glad Press N' Seal. This material is the perfect *thing for covering wounds before going into the shower. It sticks well to itself (not so well to skin), but if you can get a double layer togaed around yourself, it will keep you dry. We have bought 17 rolls.*

My love to you all, and my thanks for your continued support, kind words, cards, letters, CDs, and surprise packages. I feel quite blessed to have you all as friends and family.

Till tomorrow...

P.S. From Eileen

Let me tell you, the Leamys are going to leave here not only in remission, but totally buff. Harry set not only a personal best, but also a floor record with that 2 miles today. As for myself, I don't want to be walking down to the lake our first day home and have Harry say, "You mean to tell me I went through chemo AND your butt fell, TOO?!" So I went up to the gym on the 10th floor and did a little running. I'm proud to say, I lapped everyone there. Of course, most of them were hampered by the weight of the oxygen tanks they had to drag along behind themselves, but HEY - I'm still calling it a victory! You are ALL so wonderful. I know from experience how hard it is to be away, but it's all good. Harry gets strength from picturing you all in your normal daily lives. Just think of us as being on Apollo 13, on the far side of the moon, slingshotting our way back to Earth.

I love you all and thank God daily for you. :)

The Daily Leamy Blog - Tuesday, October 24, 2006
(Eileen still typing)
One and all,

Following a mostly sleepless night, I have been somewhat foggy during the entirety of this day. I received antibiotics and will apparently continue to receive them intravenously to keep the bacteria in my blood at bay. I likewise expect similar issues to arise from bacteria that migrate from the skin to the colon, so I am now Mr. Superflosser-Brusher-Rinser, and as my counts continue to fall, will become even more vigilant. White cells today = 0.4, normal is 4.3. I am getting there! I did manage a 2 mile walk today, and in fact, it felt good. Now I am showered, dressed in fresh, clean pajamas, and in bed for the night with Eileenie soon to be by my side. We will pray the rosary together as we do every night for my health and the welfare of all of you.

Till tomorrow...

The Daily Leamy Blog - Wednesday, October 25, 2006
(Eileen typing)

Thank you for your praise regarding my walking. As it happens, the doctor and nurses believe I have been overdoing it, and I have been ordered to cut back, and so I shall (from E. - Dr. O'Rourke said, "You're doing so great, but now you need to coast a little bit."). Today, my white count dropped to 0.3, my hemoglobin to 10.5, and platelets to 7, so I received a platelet transfusion this afternoon. Also this afternoon, Eileen and I made it OUTSIDE to a beautiful garden of Eden type courtyard of the hospital where we enjoyed beautiful sunshine, a gentle, cool breeze, and one another. We tarried there and spoke of many things, mostly normal life. We are anxious to get back to our normal life, and will be appropriately thankful when we do.

From Eileen. - Last night our wonderful Nurse Nancy really laid down the law - in her own kind way - with Harry to get him to see that although there are many times when exercising as he has been is a good thing, this is the time when his body needs all his resources for the battle going on inside him. He and I both had trouble sleeping last night. She tried getting us both down at about 9:00, but by 11:00, we were both wide awake again like a couple of 3 year olds. Harry called her back in to give him something more to help him sleep, so she turned on a TV channel that had soothing music and pictures of stars, gave me a back rub, said, "Good night, sweethearts," and turned the lights out for the second time. I felt like Wendy and Peter Pan. The garden *today was really lovely, and it helped Harry enormously to be untethered and free, breathing the clean, cool air. We considered making a dash for the car (surely you can buy all this stuff over the internet, right?), but came back to our "dorm" room instead. I'm still second guessing that decision.*

Love to all of you.

The Daily Leamy Blog - Thursday, October 26, 2006
Hello dear hearts and gentle people,

Harry asked me to do the blog tonight since he's quite tired. Not to worry. Today he got 2 units of red blood cells, and the infection seems to be better. The transfusion took most of the day and was preceded by a big hit of Benadryl to guard against his having an allergic reaction to the red blood cells. Remember how Harry and I have always said we knew each other from day one, and haven't really had any surprises since we've been married? Well, I'm surprised. Harry flying on IV primo Benadryl (and a hit off the magic pain pump next to him) is quite the Oscar Hammerstein. I was on my Aerobed® working on my needlepoint (finally started it, Laura), when Harry burst into a little spontaneous song that went like this:

> *I'm feeling very floaty,*
> *But I love you still.*
> *You're my sweet petunia,*
> *And I'm your daffodil.*

Followed by a big, dopey grin. A little later, he extemporized the following Ode to Benadryl:

> *Oh, we all stand for Benadryl.*
> *It's a rare and wonderful little pill.*
> *Oh, it makes you very sleepy,*
> *But then you have to pee pee,*
> *So then you have to stand for Benadryl.*

Tonight, after the infusion was finally finished, we went outside and said a rosary in the front on the benches where John, Jen, Phaedra and I sat. He then walked back to the front of the building, and I wheeled him back upstairs. He is now sleeping like a baby on the nice, new striped sheets that Jen sent.

The Eucharistic minister just came - what a beautiful end to this lovely day.

I love you all and thank you so much. You have no idea how lifted we both feel.

Love,
E

Harry and I had had our dress rehearsal nearly two years before when he had his knee surgery, and we failed miserably. Then, nothing seemed at stake. Now everything was at stake.

Our hour had come.

God finally had our full attention.

"Don't cry. I'm not going to leave you."
- Harry

~ ICU ~

Friday, October 27, 2006 was cold and rainy. Harry had had a terrible night, a shocking night. He started violently vomiting at about 1:30 a.m. and continued spewing vomit and diarrhea throughout the night. All the waste his poor body disgorged was highly toxic, and the nurses and I had to continually don masks, gowns, and gloves to clean up Harry, swab the floor, and change the bed linens. Many times through the night, Harry seemed just at the edge of consciousness. The nurses tried to stave off the worst of it with Benadryl for the nausea and an IV drip for the dehydration. After several hours, there seemed to be nothing left to come out, and Harry was finally able to rest. As daylight broke, he even asked me to help him into the bathroom, so he could wash his face and brush his teeth. It looked as though the worst was over.

Still shaky myself, I went down to the cafeteria in my pajamas and got a cup of coffee. When I came back up to the room, Harry was sleeping fairly comfortably. I sat watching him and drinking my coffee until he awoke about an hour later and smiled at me.

"How are you feeling?" I asked somewhat warily.

145

"Better," he assured me. "Come in the pocket."

So I went over and lay down beside him with my head on his chest, in the crook of his shoulder, and we both dozed off. When I awoke, Harry was still sleeping, so I quietly got up, changed into my clothes, and tiptoed out of the room. I stopped at the cafeteria for another cup of coffee, put up the hood on my jacket, and went out in the rain to sit in The Green Bubble in the parking lot and make some phone calls. I first called Bill Plummer and told him what had happened. Bill was not one to give false hope, so I knew if he had anything good to say, I could count on it. Bill listened to the events of the night, but could not really advance any opinion about the situation. Unsettled, I then called Harry's son, John, to give him an update. John was so kind and understanding, I couldn't hang onto the facade I was trying to maintain and finally started to cry. I felt terrible crying on the phone to John like that, but his strength made it possible for me to let go a little. We finally said good-bye, and I took a couple deep breaths of the rainy air and went somewhat less shakily back into the hospital. I didn't want Harry to see me looking wobbly, so on the elevator, I gave myself a pep talk, slapped my cheeks for a little color, and put on a mask of calm. I stepped out of the elevator, turned to go down the hallway to Harry's room, but stopped dead at what I saw.

Telling you this, even now, makes my throat tighten and my hands shake.

There standing outside Harry's room looking in were two nurses and a priest.

They called a priest.

It was the sight of the priest that undid me. My legs gave out, and I sank to the floor in a heap. The nurse at the desk came running, hugged me, and said,

146

"No, no! He's not dead! He's still alive! We have to move him, though."

As she and I sat there on the floor, I saw the end of a gurney coming out of Harry's room as they rushed to get him to the ICU, the priest running along beside him. I struggled to my feet just as they got to the elevator. I took Harry's hand, and in the same way Harry had spoken to me so many times before, I said,

"Don't worry, my loveperson. Everything's going to be all right," with the only smile I could manage.

Harry smiled weakly, squeezed my hand, and closed his eyes.

They let me ride down in the elevator, but then told me I had to wait while they got him into the ICU. The priest led me gently by the arm to the waiting area and quietly sat with me. I could see he was trying to think of something to comfort me.

"You really love him a lot," was how he started.

I didn't see where he was going yet and could only manage a nod.

"Sometimes loving a person means letting them go."

He launched into a revery about how he would handle it if he were in Harry's situation. He said he thought he'd like to take a trip to a tropical island and spend whatever time he had left drinking beer on the beach.

Now I saw where he was headed, and I didn't want to go there with him. I was not ready to go there. I was miles from there. As he kept talking, denial took the reins, and all my adrenaline and terror turned into anger. Anger aimed squarely at him. All I could do was tune him out and try not to scream at him. It was so much better than thinking about what might be happening to Harry.

Finally, I don't know how long later, they let me see Harry for just a moment. He was unconscious. The only information they would give me at that point was that back on the fifth floor, his blood pressure had plummeted, and they could barely find a pulse. Then they said it was time for me to leave, so they could work on Harry, but that when Dr. O'Rourke got to the hospital, he would let me know what was happening.

I walked out of the hospital back into the rain, went to the car, and started spreading the shocking news.

After I called everyone, I had no idea what to do. I thought Harry was only going to be in the ICU a day or two, so I went back up to the room on the fifth floor where we had been since he entered Saint Francis on October 9, 18 days prior. The nurses said I could sleep in the room that night, but that I would have to move our things out the next day. Letting me stay there was a kindness on their part, but I still didn't understand what was happening, and I almost didn't want to know. I lay down on my Aerobed® trying to take in everything that had happened. Finally, I was able to get up and go back to the ICU. By that time, Dr. O'Rourke had arrived at the hospital. Dr. O'Rourke always had a calming effect on Harry and me, but this time there wasn't much good medically to say at the moment. What he was able to say was that Harry's collapse was not unexpected, and then he gave me the thought I could hold onto, the hope that helped me through that night. He put his hand on my shoulder and said,

"Having him walk out of here is still the plan."

That was all I needed to hear. I didn't need numbers or charts or analysis. I just needed hope.

I went back up to the fifth floor, got my wits about me, and blogged,

The Daily Leamy Blog - Friday, October 27, 2006
Hello All,

Today there was some good news, which was that Harry's blood is now free of blast cells. This is the first indication that the chemo has been working effectively.

However, because of the side effects of the chemotherapy - nausea, etc. - Harry has become dehydrated with low blood pressure. This has been the main cause of a lot of his discomfort. He had somewhat of a bad night last night, and the nurses decided to move him to the ICU. Mainly, they want to monitor the staph infection and the consequent fever.

The nurses insist that this is not uncommon and should not cause concern. We take them at their word. Please remain faithful in your prayers and hopeful in your thoughts.

Love to you all,
The Leamys

Saturday, October 28, the first family member to arrive was Phaedra who drove down early that morning from Johnson City, Tennessee. The ICU had strict visiting hours, and I had not even been able to see Harry myself yet that morning, so Phaedra and I went to the cafeteria to get some coffee, then back up to the ICU to wait until we could see Harry. When they finally let us in, and Harry slowly came into view, he was almost unrecognizable, grotesquely swollen from a flood of 30 pounds of fluid that they had pumped into him the night before. He was still unconscious. Phaedra and I were devastated at the sight of him, but I sat next to his bed stroking his hand while Phaedra stood at the foot of the bed. He looked so battered that I couldn't keep from crying, and I just sat there holding his hand with tears streaming down my face. Slowly, he opened his eyes, looked at me, and smiled and said,

"Don't cry. I'm not going to leave you."

Calm and confident. So like himself. My Harry, my home.

Phaedra and I looked at each other and burst out laughing, giddy with relief. She had heard him, too. We both heard him clearly. We laughed so hard, we could hardly get our breath. Harry wasn't going to die. He said so himself, and we believed him.

Hearts aloft, we fairly danced down the hall and out.

Our jubilation was short lived. There was still a long way to go. John and Jennifer arrived from New York that afternoon and set about asking the doctors the hard, meticulous questions that I couldn't and didn't want to hear answered. They were looking for hope in the detailed data. I was looking elsewhere.

The lake house was nearly an hour away, so we were all staying at hotels near the hospital just in case we needed to get back there quickly. Phaedra stayed until Sunday when my sister, Christie, came from Pittsboro, North Carolina. Early every morning around 6:30, Dr. O'Rourke called from the ICU. My heart stopped every time until he said Harry was still alive.

For awhile, every morning brought a new horror. Sunday, O'Rourke said Harry was having trouble breathing, so they induced a coma in him and put him on a ventilator. Monday morning, they were considering whether to put him on dialysis. They had rehydrated him so rapidly and with so much fluid that his kidneys couldn't keep up. But there was still hope. There was an army out there praying. I continued to send out missives to the troops.

The Daily Leamy Blog - Monday, October 30, 2006

You know, when Harry and I decided to get married and retire, we planned to travel all around - Alaska, Montana, Ireland, Italy, lots of places. But virtually every trip we've made has been to visit family. Even the trip we made last spring after being in Finn-land was a "family pilgrimage" back to our roots. And for the first year after we moved to the lake when I was struggling with finding my "purpose" here and finding something "meaningful" to do here, my incredibly wise Aunt Eileen said repeatedly, "I think this family is your purpose." I didn't REALLY hear that until now. I'm starting to think that every time Harry and I have said our NEXT trip was going to be just for us, God's had a good laugh. I don't think that's His plan. God's very big on family, and we both see that when He put us together, he wasn't just putting the two of us together - he was putting ALL of us together. My aunts and uncles told us all our lives, "Family is everything." The family you're born into and the family God puts you into. Family is everything.

Harry is stable, and there have been small indicators that he is improving. One of the nurses back on our old stomping ground, the 5th floor (which we now regard as the Land of Milk and Honey) told me yesterday, "Everyone from here makes their trip to the ICU. Nobody gets by without it." So although this is serious, it is not unexpected as far as the medical team is concerned. Dr. O'Rourke told us that every 24 hours that goes by means Harry is that much more likely to walk out of here, and today was our 3rd 24 hours. More importantly, Harry's twin brother, Larry, assures me that Harry is going to pull out of this. He can feel it. Family.

I love you all.

The Daily Leamy Blog - Tuesday, October 31, 2006

Today Harry opened his eyes. Let me back up. When we got there this morning, I sent my sister Christie in first to see how things were because the first thing in the morning is always a little scary. She came back out in tears, but they were tears of joy, and said, "Eileen, he's WONDERFUL! He had the best night, and there's lots of good news!" SO! His level of sepsis is down, his urine output is good, and his kidneys are filtering, so they are holding off on dialysis. He is clearly trying to breath on his own, so they are ratcheting down the ventilator setting and decreasing his sedation to slowly get him to wake up. Miracle of miracles, he has also started making his own white blood cells - up from .2 yesterday to .4 today. All through the day, we went in in little 5 minute visits, and he clearly raised his eyebrows in an attempt to open his eyes all day but would then be exhausted by the effort and fall back asleep. Once, I started to say the Hail Holy Queen to him (one of his favorite prayers), and he started to move his lips along with me. Finally toward the end of the afternoon, I spoke to him and put my hands on his face, and he opened his big blue eyes. He was still groggy, and his eyes shut back again, but he opened them several times and clearly looked at me before going back to sleep.

So this wonderful family of faith that we are ALL part of is ripping the shingles off Heaven one by one. We're almost down to the last one.

I love you all.

The Daily Leamy Blog - Wednesday, November 1, 2006

Dear Hearts,

Today was another day of small victories. This was supposed to have been the EARLIEST day that Harry would start growing his own white blood cells, but instead, today he is at .9. That's a full 25% - only 75% more to go. His sepsis continues to lessen, and his kidneys are still holding their own. They are trying to wean him off the ventilator, and it's clear that he's trying to breath on his own, so they now give him periods when the ventilator is turned off to allow his body to get some "exercise" in breathing on his own. He once again opened his eyes several times during the day, and when I sang him the little petunia/daffodil song he wrote for me, he lifted up his arm for me to hold his hand. The nurse said that when she said, "I hear you taught Mechanical Engineering," he squeezed her hand to answer yes. When I asked him to squeeze my hand to tell me he loved me, he was too pooped to do that but did raise his eyebrows to answer. All three of his doctors are "very pleased" with his progress, so we're expecting that tomorrow will be another good day. Jill went back home today, and Christie will leave tomorrow. Yesterday Jen asked me how long Christie was staying, and I said, "She says she'll stay as long as I want," to which Jen asked, "How about as long as I want?" My wonderful, steady sister has been a source of calm and comfort for more than just me. Yet another blessing.

The Daily Leamy Blog - Thursday, November 2, 2006

Today was another banner day in the life of Harry Our Hero. Dr. O'Rourke called this morning saying, "I have lots of good news," and through the day, the news just got better and better. First, his white blood cells are now at 1.5 - almost double from yesterday. More importantly, he's clearly making good white cells because the original source of the infection is now gone. He's just fighting off some hangers on. The point is, his own body clearly kicked into gear and started fighting the infection. Second, they removed the Swan catheter that was going into his heart, so there's one less source of possible infection. His kidneys are working well enough that they felt comfortable giving him a diuretic to help get rid of the probably 20 pounds or so of edema that he's been dealing with, and he's peeing like a champ. They also started giving him a little Ensure through his feeding tube because his stomach has been making rumblings, and he seems to be tolerating that well. Finally, and best of all, he spent virtually the whole day breathing on his own, and they're talking about taking out the ventilator tomorrow morning. The ventilator is the last thing they remove, so it's a real sign of confidence that he's getting better and better. The bone marrow biopsy will be Monday or Tuesday.

I can't thank you all enough for all your support. I read your comments every night before blogging, and I really feel lifted. Tonight is my first night by myself since this started, but I'm thinking of all of you crowded into this room *watching over me and watching over Harry all night. I have a wonderful set of books called, "In Conversation with God," and last night I read a meditation entitled, "Afterwards, you will understand." We've seen many, many blessings in this already, and we know our suffering is the only path to becoming the people God wants us to be - people who love enough - agape enough - to be willing to put another's needs ahead of our own. One of the things that struck me in this meditation was the sentence, "God never makes mistakes." I love that. Nothing in this is a mistake.*

The Daily Leamy Blog - Saturday, November 4, 2006

Last night, we had a great conversation with our favorite nurse, Brian. It had occurred to me that Harry might be on a little bit of a plateau, and Brian made the point that we would probably not see the BIG daily improvements we have been seeing because he had to make those huge strides in the beginning just to survive. Now, as Brian put it, "He's come a long way, and the path to wellness is much shorter, so you're going to see smaller steps forward now." Some other quotable quotes from the nurses last night - "We're now past the 'Is he going to make it through the night' stage to the 'Wonder how much better he's going to be next week?' stage." Another nurse, Pat, nodded and said, "Yup. We're definitely over the hump." Today the oncologist described Harry as "stable," and the infectious disease doctor told me he thought it would only be another week or so in the ICU, then back to the Garden of Eden on floor 5.

Yesterday, Harry's white blood cells were at 1.8 and today they were at 2.5. They've also confirmed that there are no blast cells in the new white blood cells. I'm ready to call that remission, but the biopsy next week will tell for sure. He's got a little fever which might be any number of things, but his lungs are improving as he continues to get rid of the edema (10 lbs. worth yesterday alone). He is more alert, and clearly trying to get that blasted breathing tube out of his mouth himself, but it's unlikely that they'll remove it until Monday when all the docs return. Yesterday, they did remove two catheters, the thinking being that they no longer needed second-by-second data, and anything they put inside you is a possible source of infection. So that was good news.

Jen and John have now returned home, and I'm really enjoying the picture of John hugging on Finn (and Emily) all day tomorrow. As for me, I'm fantasizing about the great Christmas we're all going to have with so many, many miracles. And all of you are a bit of a miracle as well.
I love you all.

The Daily Leamy Blog - Sunday, November 5, 2006

Another day with good news. The pulmonary doc said Harry's lungs are "markedly" improved, and his white blood cells were up to 2.8. They wanted to let him rest today because they intend to remove the breathing tube tomorrow morning. He's getting nice, deep breaths. They'll put him through three tests tomorrow to see whether it really is time, but they're quite conservative, so I know they won't rush this.

Phaedra and I went back to the house and got the second collage today, so both are now up in his room. Whenever he finally opens his eyes and really SEES, he'll see all our faces smiling back at him.

I'm heading to bed very, very early tonight, so I'll see you tomorrow.

I love you all.

The Daily Leamy Blog - Monday, November 6, 2006

If it weren't for the fact that Harry was sleeping peacefully in an ICU bed, you'd have thought today was a normal day at the lake. This was the first day we've been by ourselves since he was admitted to the ICU, and I sat with him several hours, reading the newspaper to him, saying the rosary, reading a meditation to him, telling him about every single one of you and what's going on with you - a normal day.

Today his white blood cells are at 3.2. All the blood and sputum cultures they sent to the lab a few days ago came back negative, so he is without infection. They believe they've figured out the rash - an allergic reaction to a particular antibiotic (which has also been known to cause fever), so they took him off that one, and the rash is indeed much better. They decided to give him another day with the respirator in place, even though he's breathing on his own. They say they like to"err on the side of caution," and for that, I'm grateful. They would like him to be more alert and responsive before taking out the ventilator, so they'll see how he is tomorrow again. Removing the ventilator is the big goal each day now.

I believe you are all in the process of rescuing my husband. So I'm sitting here in my pink and daisied "Life Is Good" pajamas, certain that God's in His heaven, and all's right with the world.

Your prayers have purchased more time for me to live with the love of my life.

I love you all,
Eileen

"I prayed really, really hard for a longtime, and I was alive."
- Harry

∼ My Boyfriend's Back ∼

The *Daily Leamy Blog* - *Tuesday, November 7, 2006*
From a jubilant Eileen

My boyfriend's back
And you're gonna be in trouble
Hey la Hey la
MY BOYFRIEND'S BACK!

So I started the morning with a 7:00 a.m. phone call from the ever cautious Dr. O'Rourke who told me that things weren't looking good for removing the ventilator, and he wanted to prepare me for the possibility that they might have to surgically insert a tube in Harry's windpipe. I was in a fairly fright-ened frame of mind and launched into a special novena. I was also deter-mined to talk to them about getting Harry off all medication that made him sleepy.

But when I got to his room, there was the ventilator lying on the bed! I thought he'd taken it out himself (go, Harry), and ran to get the nurse. She said they'd decided that, since the decision was borderline, they would take it out and see how the day went. All this activity woke my sweet husband who looked at me and said in a hoarse and breathy voice, "It's good to see you."

157

He always did have a gift for understatement. His white blood cells are at 3.9, and his platelets went from 20K to 25K. He's doing so well without the ventilator, that they finally took the machine out of his room. Tomorrow the feeding tube!

So I left him with lots of kisses and the knowledge that all of you are right in the room with him.

My boyfriend's back!

The Daily Leamy Blog - Wednesday, November 8, 2006

5th FLOOR HERE WE COME! Tomorrow we ascend! A lunar launch never got this much hoopla. Today the feeding tube came out, so all that's left is to work on getting Harry's strength back and getting him even more oriented. Today he looked around and concluded he was in New Mexico. They say this is very typical and will pass in a little bit. I think the return of the lamps and quilt will go a long way toward getting him face forward again.

I think two of our kids said it best yesterday. Jessamin said, "I'm sorry that this all happened, but isn't it amazing that in the homes of all our family and friends every night everyone is talking about the miracle God is working for us?" John put it more succinctly. "It's like we get everything we ask for." Exactly.

I love you all. Harry does, too.

The Daily Leamy Blog - Saturday, November 11, 2006
Dear hearts and gentle people,

Sorry for the two day blackout. Absolutely nothing is wrong. In fact, things are going great. Larry and Donna were there for our triumphal arrival on the 5th floor. Harry was still a little disoriented and kept turning the lights on all night, so he could do "my exercises." Finally at about 3 a.m., when the lights flipped back on for the 4th time, I pointed out it was the middle of the night and asked him whether we could just keep the light off and go back to sleep, to which he answered (while pumping his arms in the air), "I'm not interested in that!! I'm interested in getting out of here. If YOU'RE interested in sleeping, go sleep someplace else!" I took my comforter and pillow to the lounge where some fellow had apparently been rousted from his wife's room as well, so he slept on the couch, and I slept spread over a chair and ottoman. The next day, Harry was complaining about the food (about time!), so he's certainly getting his wits about him. All his vital signs are excellent, and yesterday the white blood cells were at 4.9 - so good they're hardly even worth repeating anymore. He has finished out all the antibiotics, so all he has left is an IV to make sure he's hydrated. He's eating regular meals supplemented by protein shakes and can get almost anything he wants - last night he asked for a peanut butter and jelly sandwich but said today that, "It wasn't like at home." (Yes, tomorrow I'll have one from home for him.) The physical therapist got him sitting up (with help) and standing (briefly and with help) on Friday, so all that really remains right now is for him to build up his physical strength. He's more "present" everyday and today told me our phone number, address, his social security number and his birthday. He's been making jokes and even laughed out loud at a discussion we were having about the famous "ea" debate. He also asked me to bring back his PalmPilot and a Wall Street Journal tomorrow. For those of you who know him well, that says it all!

I've been feeling a sore throat coming on and so came home to sleep last night. Phaedra is here this weekend, so I'm going to be at the hospital during the day, but sleeping at home the next couple nights to get some really restful sleep. Once she goes back to school, I and my surgical mask will move back into Harry's room. Hopefully, by that time, he'll be better oriented to night and day again - a common problem for people coming out of the ICU where the lights are on all the time.

Dr. O'Rourke has been out of town since Wednesday, so I expect that when he returns on Monday, he'll decide when he'll do the bone marrow biopsy.

I'll try not to let more than a day go by again without blogging. Harry even confided to me, "I haven't been writing on the blog," with some concern. Harry Our Hero rides again.

I love you all.

The Daily Leamy Blog - Sunday, November 12, 2006

Today was another day of plenty in the life of our hero. More talking, more laughing, more singing (when we quizzed him about whether it was day or night, he burst into Cole Porter's "Night and Day"), more motion, more Harry being Harry. Phaedra asked him why we call police "cops", and that set him off on explanations of several terms. We had him doing leg and arm exercises, and when the physical therapists came, they got him out of the bed and into the chair where he sat for about 30 minutes. He told me that he's been thinking about what's important and that when he gets home, he's canceling his subscriptions to every magazine and newspaper that doesn't have the word "trout" in the title.

Tomorrow the physical therapy kicks into high gear - hopefully twice a day - and O'Rourke comes back. Full steam ahead.

Meanwhile, Mollie (our dog) is "at her post" at the lake house (as Harry likes to say), waiting for his return. She knows something's wrong, and the sight of Harry's the only thing that can make it right.

I love you all.

The Daily Leamy Blog - Monday, November 13, 2006

Today they did the bone marrow biopsy, and we should have results in the next day or two. Whatever the result, Harry will have another round of chemo. If there's no leukemia, they do a second round as insurance against anything they might not be able to detect. If there is some leukemia left, they'll do another round to kill that off. The fact that there would be a second round didn't really hit me until last Friday, and it may hit some of you pretty hard, too. But here's what Harry had to say. I asked him whether he was afraid of another round, and he said no. I asked him why not, and he said, "I was down as low as I could get, almost dead, and I prayed really, really hard for a long time, and I was alive. So that's what you do." Can't really add anything to that. That's the formula Our Hero has prescribed, and I know you're all on board with it. We've just got a little farther to go.

Harry also said there was something specific he wanted on the blog tonight. He said, "Say that you and I were lying down in the same bed for just a little minute." So there you have it. Felt good, too.

I love you all.

The Daily Leamy Blog - Tuesday, November 14, 2006

We are in the final boarding process. Harry will be home in the next few days. Today he managed to sit up in a chair twice for a total of 70 minutes. This is excellent progress. He's all but boycotting the hospital food at this point, but at least he can now drink liquids without their having been thickened first. That means coffee!

As for me, after one night back together in the room, I have again been evicted. He says he needs the night to do his "calisthenics", and that it's too hard to keep quiet all night. A man with a plan! My part of the plan is to get our home in shape and start looking into what equipment we might need here, and what agencies to call to get some help during the day (Bill and Talley, is there any agency you recommend?)

I must run and start tackling the mountain of laundry we dragged home from the hospital. Not long now!

I love you all.

The Daily Leamy Blog - Wednesday, November 15, 2006

Dear hearts,

Today is our hero's birthday which he celebrated with a cup of Starbuck's coffee and a Snickers, declaring it the best birthday meal he'd ever had. Our sleeping arrangements have once again taken a turn. Last night with me back at home and him at the hospital, we both were lonely for the other and had a hard time sleeping. At about 11:30, I almost drove back to the hospital figuring if I WASN'T going to be able to sleep, I might as well not sleep there. This morning, we agreed that sleeping apart was a very bad idea (I did not point out that it was the Birthday Boy's idea), so I'm here at the house gathering up some things, so that I can move in again tonight.

One of the things he wants is a set of his barbells so he can work on strengthening his arms. Today he walked a few steps and then sat up in the chair for an hour. Hopefully, physical therapy will come this afternoon as well. He's also getting the Foley catheter out today. That's the last thing he's tethered to, so he'll have complete freedom.

The results of the biopsy are not yet in and may not be for another day or two. They do some kind of special testing with different stains on this sample, so it takes longer.

Our plan is for him to exercise as much as he can while I come back here during the day and get things ready for his triumphal return, then go back to the hospital in the late afternoon to tuck in for the night. This will make us both feel we're making progress toward getting home with minimal wear on our nervous systems. Gotta be able to look over and see each other, or we go into the weeds.

I love you all so much!
Eileen

Even in this setting, there were moments of sweetness. Of innocence. Ever since we had been married, Harry sometimes liked to fantasize about us having a child together, even though this was no longer likely. Shortly after our marriage, he wrote me this email from his new perspective as a 20 year old newlywed:

I love you. Good morning. Did I tell you this? The urology nurse, my old pal, asked if we had children on the way yet! Well, do we?

I love you.
Your husband

I liked that fantasy, too, so I e-mailed back,

My dear loveperson husband,

It's difficult to say whether we have a child on the way. Hard to tell. I am not nauseated – a sure sign. And I am not throwing up – another sure sign. But I am missing you horribly, and were you here, would be, as Jen said of Emily, "loving on" you more than ever. All I want is to be in your arms.

Is that a sure sign? Yes, of something...

I love you, too. I will keep loving you here on Earth and wherever else I am.

Your wife

A few months later, Harry started up the game again.

My dear love scone person wife,

I saw a rainbow tonight and thought of you. I listened to the Reagan stuff on NPR, and I will admit that I cried some. He was a great man, in my opinion.

163

Now here is the thing. I read an article in Newsweek that contained the following mail from Ronnie to Nancy while traveling to New York:

"Eight million people in this pigeon crap encrusted metropolis (NYC), and suddenly I realized I was alone with my thoughts, and they smelled sulfurous. Time was not a healer. When dinner time finally arrived, I walked down to '21' where I ate in lonely splendor. It was at this point with self-pity coming up fast on the rail that you joined me. Yes, you and I had a roast beef. Wanting only half a bottle of wine, we were somewhat restricted in choice, but we politely resisted the huckstering of the wine steward and settled for a '47 Pichon Longueville'. It was tasty, wasn't it? We walked back in the twilight, and I guess I hadn't ought to put us on paper from thereon. Let's just say I didn't know my lines this morning. Tonight we'll eat at the hotel, and you've got to promise to let me study... at least for a little while. I suppose some people would find it unusual that you and I can so easily span 3,000 miles, but in truth, it comes very naturally. Man can't live without a heart, and you are my heart, by far the nicest thing about me and so very necessary. There would be no life without you, nor would I want any."

Wow, no wonder I admired the man. I wish that I had written something even remotely like this to you. Instead, let me simply say that you are my life and my love.

I learned from the Newsweek article that the Reagan's 1st child was born 7 months after their wedding. He knocked her up! Way to go, Ron!

Can I knock you up? Well, as Ronnie would say, I can try.

I love you terribly and eternally.
H

A couple years later, we were in New Jersey visiting Harry's grandson, Finn, who was a few months old. One morning, Harry was happily feeding Finn breakfast when he stopped, spoon in mid air, turned to me, eyes twinkling, and smiled, "We should have one of these." Several months later, his brother and sister-in-law were visiting us at the lake house, and we were talking about my lack of energy. His brother teased, "Gee, Eileen, maybe you're pregnant." Harry grinned at me and asked, "Well are you?" So this was a happy fantasy that he played with every now and then.

That being the case, I guess what happened in the hospital was not surprising, but it was a wonderful moment that transported us both back into that playful joy we'd had. Coming out of the ICU, Harry had what they referred to as "ICU psychosis". He had no concept of day and night. Time was all the same. He had visions during the day and wild, vivid dreams every night. These dreams always had some kernel from an event in the "real" world. For example, he still had a lot of difficulty controlling his bladder. He was aware of the sensation of urinating, but he didn't always know why. One night he had a distressing dream of an enormous Christian diorama that had been set on fire by terrorists, and he alone had to put out the fire by peeing all over it like a fire hose. His dreams were vivid and lifelike to him.

One afternoon, a lovely young nurse who was pregnant was on duty, and we had an amicable afternoon as she came in and out. That night, I was awakened when Harry turned on the light, excitedly calling to me,

"Eileenie!! Why didn't you tell me?!"

There was my sweet husband, blissfully beaming.

"Tell you what?" I asked sleepily.

"That we're having twins!" he happily exclaimed.

He'd had a wonderful dream that I was pregnant with twins, and he

165

was over the moon.

It put a lump in my throat to see how overjoyed he was. For a brief, shining moment, his fantasy came true. We were young and in love with a glorious life ahead of us.

As Harry liked to say, there were "miles and miles of skyward hope above."

"We won't take this for granted."
- Harry

∼ Remission ∼

The Daily Leamy Blog - Saturday, November 18, 2006
God's Hat Trick - From Eileen

Trust me when I tell you to sit down. Now hold onto the arms of the chair.

Harry is in remission.

Let's just let that sink in for a minute...

As you know, we've been waiting for the results of the bone marrow biopsy for a week. Yesterday, a very frustrated Dr. O'Rourke came in at about 8:00 a.m. and said the results were still not in. He did, however, enumerate the 3 possible outcomes - no change, remission, or some leukemia cells still floating around - and told us he thought it would probably be the third possibility. Harry had a pretty bad night with lots of tossing and turning and violent nightmares. This morning, O'Rourke's partner, Dr. Spitzer, came in and said, "So how about that biopsy?" We said, "Yeah, we're STILL waiting for the results." Spitzer said, "What are you talking about? I just read the report. It's clear." To which, in our typically calm and understated fashion, we both yelled, "WHAT?!?!" Spitzer was having a really jolly time by now and said to Harry, "I'll show your wife the report," and to me, "Hurry up. I'll

167

show you the report." Not that he was thrilled or anything. Now those of you who know me know I'm the last person in the family that anyone would invite to look at a medical report. But we fairly ran down the hall to look at it, and Spitzer underlined the phrase that said, "No (blah blah blah) and/or (blah blah blah) evidence of residual/recurrent acute leukemia." He then went on to say, "Now, even though he's in REMISSION, he'll still need some followup chemo. Like weeding a garden. You get all the weeds you can see, but you still spray, so they don't come back." I was still in shock and said, "Let me get this straight. Here's what O'Rourke said yesterday, and he said he thought it would be option 3." Spitzer just smiled and said, "This is better."

The Daily Leamy Blog - Sunday, November 19, 2006

Harry told me yesterday that one of the nurses stopped by to congratulate him on his remission, saying, "I knew this was going to happen, though." He asked her how she knew, and she thought for a moment and said, "Because you wanted it so much." Amen to that.

We both had long naps today. Lots of fatigue in both our bones. It was nice to read a book and fall asleep - to do something "normal."

Last night, Harry said a very simple prayer on both our behalves. "Thanks, God. We won't take this for granted, and we'll spend the rest of our lives doing whatever it is You want us to do." Sacrament of marriage. The three of us together.

I love you all.

Sweet dreams, Harry.

Thank you, God

"Every day we need to...do something for God."
- Harry

~ Back Home After Round One ~

We are, all of us, on-campus students at the School of Trust. Mary teaches the master class daily in Cana. At the wedding at Cana, Jesus turns matrimony into a sacrament. His mother turns trust into an art form. Her approach is deceptively simple. Just two steps. Step one:

"They have no wine."

First, go directly to Jesus and tell Him the problem. Don't panic, don't flail around trying to fix things on your own. Don't gather a gaggle of opinions from everyone you know. Don't worry about coming up with possible solutions. You can't think of anything He hasn't already thought of, anyway. Just hand Him the problem. Then, in the last words of Mary's ever recorded, she gives us step two:

"Do whatever He tells you."

Not, "Hear Him out and then decide whether His idea will work." Not, "Listen to what He says and decide whether you agree." Not even, "Wait and see if He even answers. He may or He may not."

No.

"Do whatever He tells you."

She trusts that He will do something. It doesn't matter what. Whatever He does will be the most wonderful, most powerful solution possible for the problem.

So she sits back down and finishes her wedding cake.

Trust.

In November of 2006, toward the end of Harry's first round of chemotherapy, the problem was that Harry was still quite weak. The doctors thought he needed another couple weeks of physical therapy before we could take him home, but they could not keep him at Saint Francis for rehabilitation. Harry and I were discouraged, and I saw how weak he was. I was terrified that if we went home now, something horrible would happen on my watch, and he would fall and break an arm, a leg, a hip, something, and he would not be able to heal. I was physically sick at the thought. But I also believed that the lake was the best place for him to recuperate. I didn't know what to think, what to pray for.

Rehab facilities are almost always at nursing homes. The rehabs in Greenville were no exception. I spent a couple days visiting every nursing home Greenville had to offer. At that time, most of the facilities were dreary and depressing. Most of the patients were considerably older and more feeble than Harry and were there with no hope of reprieve. I walked into one place, and the stench of urine was so strong, I turned right around, went back in our car, and cried. Even the best of the lot was still clearly just a last stop before death. Worst of all, even in the most acceptable facility, I would not be able to stay in Harry's room with him. Even if I went to see him every day, I knew he would not do well at all without me being there day and night. I was very worried that if Harry went into rehab, we would lose all the forward momentum we had worked so hard to achieve, and he would become lethargic. I knew home was the only place where he had any hope of thriving. I was quite demoralized. Distracted by despair. I did not want to alarm anyone, least of all Harry, so I kept quiet.

The Daily Leamy Blog - Thursday, November 16, 2006
Dear hearts,

Yesterday and today were big days. Harry's big birthday present was getting the Foley catheter out and having the freedom to pee into a plastic bottle! He said, "I finally feel like I have control over SOMETHING!" Today he was able (with the help of a walker and a therapist) to walk around the bed and back to his chair. Tomorrow the hallway!

Tonight Harry and I were chiding ourselves for allowing any worry or fear to enter our minds. Harry had the antidote. Our Hero said, "Every day we need to look for an opportunity to do something for God." So here's something for God today. Thank you, Father. Thank you, Father. Thank you, Father.

I love you all.
Eileen

My optimism was short-lived, however. Even with the young, attentive, physical therapists at Saint Francis, it didn't seem to me that Harry was making all that much progress. In a nursing home, what was already an uphill battle for him would be akin to Kilimanjaro. I was living in dread of what was coming.

God had everything in hand, though.

The Daily Leamy Blog - Monday, November 20, 2006

According to the nursing staff, I "look good." I feel pretty good, and while I

171

know that I need lots of physical therapy, I want to get on with it. Eileen and I have changed our focus from finding a rehab facility to doing rehab at home where love abounds.

Love,
Harry

From Eileen---------------------------

In a wacky turn of events, the staff discovered that the "plush" rehab will not take cancer (even former) patients. They're afraid the person will suddenly require some of those "expensive" chemo type drugs, and they don't want to run the risk of incurring that cost. I have no doubt the place up the road that smells of urine would have no such issue, but we have a much better alternative that has a gorgeous view of a lake. So now they've lit a fire under the hospital physical therapists and made sure they were coming twice a day for an extended period. The result is that last night Harry was able to go in and use the actual bathroom, and today he walked back and forth to the nurses station twice. The therapist today said she thought Harry was only a few days away from going home, and the social worker here said, "Let's try to get you home by Thanksgiving." God clearly intends for Harry to have an entirely different type of rehab.

I love you all.

Tuesday, Nov. 21 - From Both of Us
One and all,

We have reentered the Earth's atmosphere and are about to splash down. Tomorrow, to be exact. We leave St. Francis in the morning and sleep in our own bed tomorrow night. Eileen has spent literally the entire day disinfecting every inch of the house while Harry learned to walk up a few stairs. Meaning he can get into our house. Unfortunately, even though his blood levels are going up, he is still somewhat neutropenic, so we are going to be completely *sequestered.*

Needless to say, we are very excited at the prospect of going home and stay-
ing there.

Love,
Harry and Eileen

I lied. My worst fear was coming true. I was happy for Harry that we were going home, but I was also terrified something might happen to him on my watch. I'd seen plenty of times when his fever had spiked, and his blood pressure plummeted, and I was overwhelmed by the responsibility. His being neutropenic meant he was susceptible to every little bacteria or virus out there. A microscopic bit of mold on a piece of bread could kill him. O'Rourke gave me a long list of foods Harry could not eat. All root vegetables were out. All fruit without a thick peeling, out. Fruit juice, out. He had to drink eight bottles of *bot-tled* water a day (we were on well water, a major no-no). And the range of activities he was not to do was staggering. Mustn't go near the garden. And in the name of all that is holy, stay away from the lake! All sheets and towels he touched had to be washed in hot water, bleach, and dye-free detergent, and changed daily. The list of all these land mines, they naturally assigned to me. I forgot all God had done for us and lost all perspective. I truly felt completely on my own, like I was the only thing standing between Harry and death. I couldn't get a good breath to save me. So imagine my delight with the homecoming celebration Harry secretly had planned.

They loaded us into The Green Bubble, waved good-bye, and we were on our way back home. Harry was quite tired, so we put the seat back down, and he slept the whole way home. When we got home, I got his walker out of the back and went around to his side of the car to help him out. We managed to slowly get him out of the car, up the few stairs into the house, and down the hallway that led out of the house to the lake. At this point, Harry, still a little loopy from pain meds, jauntily announced,

"I'm going to pee off the deck like a man!"

What?!?!

To my horror, off went Harry toward the sliding glass door that led out onto the deck. Freedom's siren song seduced him completely, and he abandoned his walker at the door and teetered off toward the railing. I caught his arm to steady him, and he made it to the railing, but was unused to the surgical scrubs he was wearing, so he decided to just drop his drawers entirely.

For a brief, shining moment, he was a free man, sunshine on his shoulders, peeing off the deck. But just for a moment. The adrenaline rush that propelled him now started to give out. He was suddenly spent, and he turned back toward the house. I still don't quite understand what happened next, but there I was trying to help him, there he was trying to turn and stumbling, and there, unfortunately, were the castoff scrubs down around his knees. Suddenly, he was falling face forward to the floor, half in and half out of the doorway.

I am not good in these situations. My nerves tend to come out in laughter rather than tears. After all we had been through, my nerves were running on auxiliary anyway. There was my loveperson, the love of my life, not on my watch even a full five minutes yet, face down and bottom up on the floor. It was not my finest hour. I fell to the floor and started to guffaw. Real belly laughs. I kept gasping for air and saying, "I'm so sorry. I know this isn't funny," but all I could do was lie there convulsed, half laughing, half crying.

When I finally got a grip on myself, I could see we were in real trouble. Harry was not strong enough to push or lift himself up at all. He was also not strong enough to put his arms around my neck while I tried to lift him. I couldn't drag him because he was lying on his bare stomach on the floor. The only thing I could think to do was try to roll him onto a blanket and then drag the blanket.

I got a blanket and tried to roll Harry over onto it, but he was too heavy for me, and he could not roll over himself. So I started scooching the blanket underneath him little by little and then going around to the other side of him to try to pull it through. Between scooching, pulling, and dragging him across the floor, it took me over an hour to get Harry out of the doorway, through the dining room, through our bedroom, and next to the bed. When I finally got him in position on his side of the bed, I didn't have the strength to lift him onto the bed itself. After several tries, I gave up and called our neighbor, Steve Goodwin. Steve said he'd be right down, and while we waited, I tried to pull Harry's scrubs up over his hips, but they were too far down. When Steve got there, I told him what had happened. Steve looked the situation over, bent down, lifted Harry up off the floor, and heaved him onto the bed. What a relief. Now at least he wouldn't die on a blanket on the floor.

I managed to get Harry comfortable in bed, brought him a peanut butter sandwich and a bottle of water, and sat down to blog. This is what I wrote.

The Daily Leamy Blog - Wednesday, November 22, 2006
Dear Hearts,

The Eagle has landed and is fast asleep. We're happy and relieved to be back at the lake. Tomorrow we're going to eat pie and watch movies.

Happy Thanksgiving! We're so grateful for all of your prayers and support.

Truly you have all played an important role in getting us back to our home.

175

Maybe you would have come clean. I couldn't do it, though. I did not breathe a word of what happened. I was not about to let on that Harry Our Hero was nearly undone during the first five minutes of my watch. I shut off the computer, crawled into bed next to my snoring loveperson, and prayed for all the help Heaven could muster.

The Daily Leamy Blog - December 1, 2006

Thank you for all your Thanksgiving wishes and encouragement. Even though we haven't blogged for awhile, we're still counting on your prayers and support. So why haven't we blogged in awhile? We'd love to say, as Larry hoped, that we're here drinking coffee on the deck and having a won-derful time, and we know we'll get to that point. But right now, we're both working harder than we ever dreamed. As you know, Harry was supposed to go to a rehab facility, and although he's making good progress, he still needs basically the same kind of support he was getting in the hospital with a daily doctor visit, a day nurse, a nurse's aide, a physical therapist, a dietician, a laundry service, and a night nurse. These are Eileen all rolled into one. Our typical day is lots of laundry, lots of changing the bed (especially through the night), lots of exertion getting in and out of chairs and back and forth be-tween rooms, bathing (though Harry has now devised a way to sit on the bedside commode half in/half out of the shower, and we just lather him up and hose him off - all over the bathroom!). Eileen seems to wash every towel and sheet we own every day. A visit to the doctor takes up pretty much the whole day, and last week when Harry got more red blood cells, it took from 8:30 in the morning until we got back home at 3:30. The same things that were going on in the hospital are still going on (the need for blood cells, rehy-dration, etc.), but we have to get our mojo going and get into town to do it. By the end of the day, we're both exhausted, and we're up a few times during the night.

Lest you think this picture is too dark, neither of us would rather be any-where else on the planet (including Italy). We're not complaining. These are just the practical things that need to be done when a person is recovering like

*Harry is. We don't usually talk about these things, because there's no point.
We do all this with gratitude for Harry's life, and God is giving each of us an
opportunity every day to grow in patience and humility. God loves those vir-
tues. And we're grateful to pay this small price.*

*Love,
Harry and Eileen*

*The Daily Leamy Blog - Saturday, December 9, 2006
Dear hearts,*

*Sorry for the short note last night. The blessing in yesterday was that we
woke up this morning saying, "Okay. Today, we don't spend any energy on
ANYTHING that isn't essential to maintaining our lives - and possibly getting clean underwear." In spite of yesterday, this has been a great week.
Tuesday morning, Harry said, "I think I've turned some kind of corner," and
by Heaven, he did! He started walking without the walker and started getting in and out of the shower himself - a HUGE accomplishment. He also
started getting up himself in the night to use the bathroom - another huge
accomplishment. Our visit with O'Rourke on Tuesday went better than we
could have hoped. Harry wanted to show O'Rourke a different person than
the guy he'd seen the week before, so he put on a nice black turtleneck, a black
leather jacket, and walked in under his own power. He was also sporting his
new NBA haircut. We decided the scraggly, half-lost hair look was not good,
and we shaved his head completely. Now he looks great - very sophisticated,
and like it's something he chose rather than something that happened to him.
So he was looking good for O'Rourke. Through his heroic downing of chocolate malts (heroic because everything tastes like cardboard to him), he has
gained 4 pounds, and all his "blood" counts are going up again. The upshot
of all this is that we are once again in the final boarding process for the next
round of chemo. Next Tuesday, they will do the required bone marrow biopsy
that is preliminary to the chemo. They will get the results by the next week,
and if all goes well, O'Rourke intends to get him back into St. Francis and
started on the consolidation round of chemo on or about Dec. 19. Assuming*

he is still in remission, the next round would only be 5 days of a milder chemo and 2 days of the experimental chemo, so it's not as bad as the first go round. O'Rourke also says he does "not plan for Harry to go through what he did before." I asked him what he was going to do differently, and he said, "Harry was sick before. Now he's not." Ironic that in the reunion video (thank you, Don - great as always), Harry looks healthy, but was in fact becoming critically ill. Now he looks ill (because of the ravages of the chemo), but is much more healthy and strong.

Harry wants very much to just get on with the chemo in spite of being in the hospital over Christmas (O'Rourke gave him the option of waiting until after Christmas, but he said, "Let's just do this thing."). As for myself, I can't imagine a more powerful time to be being treated than the time we commemorate the seminal event in human history - the time that God came down to the planet to live among us. The season of Advent is a time for waiting. Waiting for the arrival of the baby Jesus when all things are made new again. Waiting for the renewal of Harry's life. Of all our lives. We love you all. We offer up[1] whatever God can use from our experience for all of you. What a wonderful Christmas this will be!

Eileen

The bone marrow biopsies were particularly painful. Some of you may know that all too well. Years ago, a priest taught me the Jesus Prayer, an old Eastern Rite prayer. He told me it was very helpful in relieving pain and that it had worked especially well for him with burn patients whose pain was beyond medication. The Jesus prayer is an aspiration prayer meaning it can be used to pray without ceasing as you breath in and out. The full prayer is:

> *Lord Jesus Christ (while breathing in)*
> *Son of God (while breathing out)*
> *Have mercy on me (breathing in)*
> *A sinner. (breathing out)*

178

Whenever Harry was undergoing a bone marrow biopsy, he squeezed my hand so hard it hurt. I would gently rub his forehead as we repeated this simple prayer over and over, and after awhile, his breathing was easier, and his whole body relaxed. This prayer got him through not only biopsies, but the increasingly difficult insertion of the PICC lines that had to be snaked through a vein in his arm into his heart.

The Daily Leamy Blog - Friday, December 15, 2006

Dear hearts,

Several good things happened this week that showed that Harry is continuing to build strength and recover. On Tuesday, when the doctor did the bone marrow biopsy, he was amazed by how hard Harry's bones are. Said they were the bones of a much younger man. Chemo can soften the bones, but this has obviously not happened. Then on Wednesday, I came out of the bedroom and couldn't find him anywhere. I called his name, and he answered - FROM THE 2ND FLOOR! Said he wanted to finally get his office back in order, so there he was carrying his computer and printer back upstairs. That same day, I had to run an errand and leave with him promising to eat lunch. When I came back, I asked whether he'd eaten anything, and he answered, "Yes," but a little too hesitantly. When I asked what, he said, "A plate of cookies." Good by me! Things that he liked last week, he can't abide this week, so I was glad there was SOMETHING that sounded appetizing to him.

We're in the countdown for Tuesday's meeting with O'Rourke and expecting that we'll be heading to the hospital that day or within a couple days. Please pray that Harry is still in remission. Now after our rosary at night, we say, "Thank you for all you've given us, but we still have the audacity to ask for even more." It always feels like God smiles a crinkly-eyed smile when we say that.

Love to all you wonderful, powerful people.

The Daily Leamy Blog - Friday, December 22, 2006
One and all,

Merry Christmas from the lake! It is quiet and strangely beautiful here in the winter. We are keeping a fire in the fireplace and consuming books by the dozen. Reading voraciously was a great escape during the last week as we waited for the results of my bone marrow biopsy. Well, the results are in, and they are mixed. We had been hoping for continued remission of the leukemia, but instead got a diagnosis of "near remission," which means that only a few cancer cells were detected. We were disappointed, but subsequently learned that complete remission after only one chemo treatment is highly unlikely. Our oncologist was, in fact, quite upbeat. He said that he saw a clear path to a leukemia free life! I go into the hospital the day after Christmas to begin the next round of chemo - minus the experimental drug which they've concluded doesn't do much of anything worthwhile. O'Rourke's office called Wednesday and said I will only be getting 5 days of chemo, so that's also a relief. We are very, very optimistic about the future. O'Rourke does not say things lightly, and for him to say that a life without leukemia is a "realistic" possibility took a huge weight off us. I just need to get through the next couple rounds.

Merry Christmas to all, and to all a good night!

---

[1] "Offering it up" is the practice of offering your own physical and emotional suffering to Jesus and asking Him to add yours with His own suffering on the cross, so that He can use it for the good of others. In this way, Catholics believe all human suffering can be used for good, and no suffering needs to go to waste.

"Thank you for not leaving me."
- Harry

~ The Winter Palace ~

The day after Christmas, Harry and I returned to Saint Francis Hospital (which we now called "The Winter Palace") for his second round of chemotherapy. Harry was stoically making the best of the situation with his usual grace and humor. As for me, I was sorry he had to go through chemo again, but I was also overwhelmingly relieved not to be the only one responsible for keeping him alive. During the few weeks we had been at home, we had had one middle of the night frantic dash back to Saint Francis when Harry spiked a fever, him half-delirious, slumped against the car door, and me begging, "Not now, God. Please, not now." So I felt safer knowing someone else was monitoring him, and I could run out into the hall and get a nurse at any moment. The down side of being relieved of that terror was that all the adrenaline that had been coursing through my body for five weeks was gone. The first day after he was admitted to Saint Francis, I slept the entire night and all the next day and night. The nurses finally came and got me and took me to their little lunch room to tell me they were worried I was depressed. I thought I was just exhausted.

I set up camp for us just as I had before with quilts, lamps, books, CDs, collages, pictures, etc. We also brought my guitar. Several decades earlier, my mother had written and published a self-instructional guitar course, and Harry wanted to work through it and learn to play the guitar. We read one volume after another of Robert Parker's Spenser series, Harry throwing whichever one he'd just finished over onto my bed and saying,"Okay, hit me again." During this second chemo round, we were also able to spend more time "in the pocket", and Harry even read to me several nights. One day, I discovered Harry would eat an Italian B.M.T sub from Subway, so every morning I went out (fully garbed in a surgical mask and latex gloves so as not to catch something and bring it back to him) and bought him a sub. Harry would eat half at lunch and half in the middle of the night. Sometimes, he craved really good coffee, so I would go get some french press coffee from a nearby coffee house for him. Whatever he could manage to get down, I was happy to go and get.

The second chemo round went much better than the first, and the blog entries were fairly boring, much to everyone's great relief. By this point, word of mouth had spread, and the blog had a large following. Jessamin told me that even her father was following the blog and talking with her about what was happening. Harry's story was affecting many, many people. Their heartfelt prayers and good wishes were, in turn, also having an effect on us. There was a community of prayer, and we felt strengthened by our dear "Little Prayer Chain That Could."

The Daily Leamy Blog - Friday, December 29, 2006

Here speaks Harry with his own voice, typing with his own ten fingers. One aspect of the chemo is some nervous system damage that left my fingers with tremors just big enough to cause typing to be difficult. Now, this has subsided, and I am pleased. This blog has been typed by Eileen and Phaedra these last weeks, and I am glad to be able to contribute again.

Herewith, some actual news. Dr. O'Rourke stopped in this morning with the printout of the bone marrow biopsy from December 19. It showed 4-5% of blast (cancer) cells and contained the comment: *"Given the history of acute myelogenous leukemia status post-treatment, these findings may indicate minimal residual AML."* Per O'Rourke, this means that most of these remaining cancer cells are "left overs" from the earlier treatment and are not actively dividing. This view was bolstered by a report from this Tuesday's biopsy also. While the complete report is not in, microscopic examination of the marrow showed NO cancer cells. Again, per O'Rourke, "In oncology and horseshoes, close counts." He reported himself to be even more positive than he was when we met with him in his office. We welcomed this news joyfully and are grateful to all of your support and prayers. You are a part of this, too.

I have passed the 72 hour mark on Chemo II and look forward to getting the last two days out of the way. Then, we wait for my white cell counts to drop to zero, then climb back up to a safe level, then off to home! This cycle takes 3 weeks, and so I must wait. I am looking forward to that moment. Eileen is here with me, and we have made this room as much like home as possible, but it lacks a view of the lake, a fireplace, and our own stuff, arranged as we would like it.

Eileen asked me if I had been thinking about my rock wall project, and I had to confess that, yes, I was. This project was halted at the halfway mark by the leukemia diagnosis and is a very physical one. I am building a stacked stone retaining wall and would love to finish it by spring. Well, maybe I will.

Love,
Harry

The next day, the complete report was in, and O'Rourke told us the good news that Harry was, in fact, once again in remission. It was an incredible way to go into the New Year. I wrote to God in my journal:

I thought You were far away, but I was the one far away. When I'm by myself, not distracted by anything, You are all I think about. When I was alone in the car thinking of You, You seemed so quiet, but I felt as though You were

183

there in Heaven with Your arms crossed, looking down at us and just smil-
ing. That night, Mary, the Eucharistic minister (who shines and glows so)
came and said to Harry, "Harry, may God continue to shower you with His
smile." Then the next day, O'Rourke told us about the biopsy looking like
Harry was actually in remission.

Thank You for Your forgiveness.
Thank You for Your love.
Thank You for Harry's life.

On New Year's Day, with grateful hearts, we wrote;

The Daily Leamy Blog - Monday, January 1, 2007

Happy New Year to everyone! We are so happy and relieved to be going into
the New Year officially in remission!

Harry will stop chemo treatment today around 7 pm. He's feeling so good
now that he asked for some WD-40 to fix the squeak on the door to the
nurse's station. Same old Harry.

Over the next couple of weeks, his blood levels are expected to drop. This time
next week, they will probably be at their lowest. Once they rise again, we will
be back at the lake house.

Hope you are having a wonderful New Year's Day!

The Daily Leamy Blog - Friday, January 5, 2007

We remain on track by every measure. Today, my platelet count dipped below
the threshold for good health, and I received a unit of these essential cells. I
am sure that I will need some reds soon. Regardless, I feel fine and am getting
lots of excellent care from the staff here. One of the nurses in particular pro-
vided us both with a big helping of hope by telling us that her husband was

in chemo for 2 solid years, that they were told they would not be able to have children, and that he wasn't even expected to live. Today, he has been leukemia free for 8 years, and they have a beautiful 2 year old son, and a 9 month old daughter. They did learn right before Christmas, however, that their son is autistic, so we'd like to ask "The Little Prayer Chain That Could" (LPCTC) to add this family to your prayers. They have been a wonderful example of faith to all their family and friends. Let's all of us please ask God to provide them with the strength and grace to carry this new cross.

We continue to be amazed at how fleeting our memories are. How easy it is to forget all there is to be grateful for and to get distracted by the things we see around us - whether the lunch was what you wanted or not, whether the nurse got here soon enough, whether our library here will hold out until we're sprung, etc. That's the constant challenge of living on two planes at the same time. When we're no longer in a time of terror and on our knees, the world we see is the world we look at. We're trying to make it a habit every morning of listing all the things we have to be grateful for - to turn our eyes the right direction from the start of the day. Eyes up. Always up.

Love,
Harry and Eileen/Pop and Mamacita

The Daily Leamy Blog - Sunday, January 7, 2007

Today my heart is just overflowing - can't say why except that I've had wonderful conversations with both my sisters and my Aunt Eileen. All their voices lifted me right up. I said to Aunt Eileen, "Won't we have fun in Heaven?" and she said, "Yes! Just remember to bring your guitar. I know you can't bring your piano, but bring the guitar." We have had a good day - maybe the first day we've had here that we spent entirely in the PRESENT tense. Our only problem is that Harry has now ripped through all 36 of the Robert Parker "Spenser" mysteries. Must remember to write Robert Parker and tell him how wonderfully diverting his books have been.

Harry is doing great. We're icing the knee every hour, and that seems to be keeping it from getting any worse - perhaps even made it a little better. His counts are about the same - near the bottom - but he still shows no sign of infection. O'Rourke is back tomorrow, so it will be good to see "our guy."

Before Harry and I were married and just e-mailing around with each other, I would sometimes be reading something wonderful in the middle of the night and have to get up and e-mail him whole pages of whatever I was reading, always starting out with, "Listen to this... ." That's how I feel right now with you all. Last week I didn't get a chance to write much about the New Year, so I want, belatedly, to share this with you now. This is from the "In Conversation with God" series written by Francis Fernandez that I've quoted from before. This is from a meditation on New Year's Eve. Listen to this...

"What do most people mean by Happy New Year? Doubtless they mean a year free from illness, pain, trouble or worry; that you make plenty of money...and that news is good every morning. In short, that nothing unpleasant may happen to you. It is good to wish these material good things for ourselves and others so long as they do not make us veer away from our final goal. The new year will bring us our share of happiness and our share of trouble, and we don't know how much of each. A good year for a Christian is one in which both joys and sorrows have helped him to love God a little more. It is not a year that comes, supposing it were possible, full of natural happiness that leaves God to one side. A good year is one in which we have served God and our neighbor better, even if, on the human plane, it has been a complete disaster. For example, a good year could be one in which we are attacked by a serious illness that has been latent and unsuspected for many years, provided we know how to use it for our sanctification and that of those close to us. Any year can be the best year if we make use of the graces that God keeps in store for us and which can turn to good the greatest misfortunes. For the year just beginning, God has prepared all the help we need to make it a good year."[1] I say we've just had a very good year, and I wish us all an even better year to come.

Yep, we have complications.

First, O'Rourke told us that we could come home and just get blood checks done in Seneca. We were happy at the prospect of being at home but still a little apprehensive about the prospect of getting back to Greenville if I should develop a temperature, etc. So, yesterday Eileen and Phaedra filled the car with the Aerobed® and Eileen's clothing and went home in anticipation that I would join them today. As it happened, I recorded a temperature of 99.0 at 4 a.m., and my white cell count dropped from 900 to 800 as well. This was enough for O'Rourke to cancel our move back to the lake house. This is actually not complicated, and we were happy with his decision because it left us near caregivers if things got worse.

Second, Dr. Jennings stopped in this afternoon and told us that the lab culture results done on the fluid that he took from my knee were positive. You all will remember that my right knee has become swollen and painful and has remained so even while I have taken things easy for the last month. The positive result was for a Gram--positive bacteria that may have taken up residence in the prosthesis or on the surface of same. We will know more after more lab work. So, Jennings has ordered a Vancomycin IV drip to try and go after this bug. Again, we shall see.

What all of this means is still very much an open question that will be answered only with time. Of course, as time passes we will keep you all informed via this blog.

We rely on your prayers, prayers for us, for the doctors and nurses, and all of the other people whose efforts are essential in running the rather amazing health care system that we are enjoying.

There was a wolf at the door that we did not notice, however. Harry's knee started to become more and more of a problem. Little did we know how big that problem would eventually turn out to be.

The Daily Leamy Blog - Sunday, January 14, 2007

Dear Hearts,

Leukemia remains at bay, and this round of chemo is doing much less damage to my body and mind. I still have chemo brain, but at a much lower level, am able to type this post, and generally feel pretty terrific, except for the knee, which remains sore and swollen, and as I mentioned in a previous blog, is infected with a low virulence bug.

The bug that has taken up residence in and around the prosthesis in my right knee has a name. Its name is coagulate negative staphylococcus. This particular bug is not destroyed by oral or IV antibiotics, the reason being that it sticks to the surface of the foreign material and just cannot be reached. The standard way of treating a prosthesis that is contaminated in this way is to remove it, thoroughly cleanse and disinfect the wound, then put in a new one. In the case of knees, the standard treatment is to put in a temporary splint, let the patient recover, then do the normal knee job.

Well, as I write, my white cell count is less than 1, and I cannot undergo surgery. The staph is being treated with 4 antibiotics, and they expect that this will be sufficient to keep me free of other infections until my immune system regains its strength. After this is accomplished, we will entertain more serious discussions with the doctors about the knee. Naturally, the knee business will add some time to the whole process, but this is a commodity that we have in excess.

From Eileen-------
Today, as you might imagine, has been a bit of a mental setback, so we have been listing positive aspects of this knee issue. First, there is NOT a second infection as was feared in Harry's blood. Second, the 2 knee surgeries are

done six weeks apart, so there's not a lengthy recovery of many months followed by a second surgery. Third, this is not life threatening. It is just something that has to be taken care of.

We continue to read books all day (thanks, John, for the Lee Childs recommendation). If any of you have recommendations for a good mystery series - 30 installments minimum! - lay it on us. We also continue to lie in Harry's bed and pray the rosary every night around 8. This is the best part of the day. It reminds us both of why we married each other and that God put us together. Don and Jeanne, you wrote about us winning back our freedom. This experience is giving us our true freedom. The freedom and comfort of finally believing in Divine Providence. What is that passage in the Bible? "Lord, we believe. Please help our unbelief."

With love to you all,
Eileen

The Daily Leamy Blog - Monday, January 15, 2007
Dear hearts,

What a good day we've had! Last night, while we were doing the rosary, I just kept saying, "Help. Help." This morning it came in the form of a phone call to Harry from Dr. Fehring in Charlotte (who put Harry's knee in). Harry told Tom everything, and it turns out Tom is the one who came up with the "gold standard" (in Dr. Bowers' words) of the dual-surgery approach to infection in an artificial joint. BUT! He told Harry he thought there were a couple of other approaches he might try (I say he, because he said, "My rule is if I put it in, I take it out.") that are not nearly as invasive or traumatic. You can imagine the uplifting effect this had on us (probably the same effect it's having on you). Then Dr. Jennings came in and said he'd been thinking about Harry's knee all weekend and thought it was best to keep managing it with antibiotics for awhile. Harry told Jennings about his conversation with Tom, and Jennings was very enthusiastic about working/consulting with Tom any way they could. So Jennings is going to call Fe-

hring and work this out with him. We are tremendously relieved. I don't know what Fehring will come up with, but I feel sure it will be something much easier than what we've been told up to now.

So we went outside to the garden to get some fresh air and decided that to-morrow we'll have a little picnic out there at lunchtime. What is it about the smell of the air that makes you feel so alive? Harry really basked in the sunlight. Our hero has not been out of this room since a couple days after we got here, but has somehow managed to keep his sanity - and even his sense of humor.

So we're still in our 7 1/2' x 8 1/2' cubicle, but feeling much better about things. Harry may have to start building some bookshelves pretty soon, though, or the nurses aren't going to be able to get into the room. I was cleaning up the ever present clutter on my side of the room when I looked at the clock and surprised myself by thinking, "Oh good! It's only 7:30." I was happy to have gotten a little housekeeping done and still have plenty of time to read a new book I picked up for $3.00 today - E.L. Doctorow's "The March." Like the old Roger Miller song says, "You can't roller skate in a buf-falo herd, but you can be happy if you've a mind to."

God gave me another bit of help in the form of our sweet nurse Margaret last night. She knew we'd had a rough day, and so when she came in about 10 that night, I saw her writing something on a paper towel that I thought was just medical note taking. Instead, she handed the paper towel to me as she went out. Here's what she wrote -

> *The light of God surrounds us*
> *The love of God enfolds us*
> *The power of God protects us*
> *The presence of God watches over us*
> *Wherever we are*
> *God is.*

Amen to that. I love you all.

We had a lovely anniversary yesterday - actually felt a little celebratory. We tried to block out this room and look at each other, at least for a moment, with the same eyes we did 3 years ago at Our Lady of Lourdes. That whirlwind was such a happy time, we felt lucky to have such great memories to replay. One of the nurses went and got the "music therapist" who came and sang a very lovely rendition of "Stand By Me" (fully gowned in yellow Tyvek and mask), and the nursing staff gave us two Hershey bars and a bag of cinnamon honey pretzels with a lovely card signed by virtually all the staff. Very sweet.

Harry spent the night free of fever and believed that the knee had improved. It could be more confidently used to hobble to the toilet and seemed to hurt less at rest. The rationale for this is that the infection that caused the original fever is one and the same that caused swelling of the knee. They have been pumping antibiotics by the bucket full to fight this since last Friday and will continue to for another 2 weeks (we don't know how much of that will be here or at home). This got rid of the fever and now seems to be working on the knee swelling. Maybe this will get him well enough to live with the knee as it is! If so, we'll take it.

We continue to pray for all of you, for the doctors and nurses here, for specific individuals that we have met on this journey. Of course, we continue to pray for Harry's complete cure and a life free of cancer.

The day before our anniversary, Harry had blogged that he wished we could be in a more romantic setting, so he could show me how much I meant to him, but that, "The same trite phrases said by the same bald guy will probably have to do." What we did not say on the blog was what, on the night of our anniversary, as I lay next to Harry "in the pocket", Harry My Hero said to me. He did not say any of those "trite phrases" he thought he might have to use. He said something completely new that he had never said before.

191

"Thank you for not leaving me."

I was completely taken aback. I raised myself up on my elbow to look him in the eyes and asked,

"What in the world are you talking about?"

"A lot of women would have left."

I saw by the fact that Harry would not look at me how tender a thought this was for him. I pondered for a moment before I responded. There were several things I could say, all good and true. I could say, "None of those women get to be married to you," or I could say, "None of those women are crazy in love," or even, "I'm not like any of those women." What I did say was the most powerful, the most wonderful, the most meaningful answer I knew.

"I'm your wife."

Harry nodded, teary-eyed, and kissed my forehead.

The Daily Leamy Blog - Tuesday, January 23, 2007

Dear Hearts,

Tomorrow, after 28 days here at our Winter Palace, we are going home (my fingers are crossed). My blood is improving daily and the swelling in my knee is shrinking too. I will be taking antibiotics via an IV every day at home but have been assured that this is not at all difficult. The antibiotics regime will last until the end of February, at which time the docs will all confer as to the next steps. I will, at that time, also have another bone marrow biopsy to determine that the leukemia is still in remission. Well, that is the news. We will post this blog weekly beginning next Wednesday unless something genuinely newsworthy happens, at which point we will post a special edition.

For now, we are grateful for the prospect of 5 weeks at home in our own space, for your continuing support, and for one another.

Love,
Harry

We had been debating with O'Rourke about whether it was safe to go home, and sure enough, the very next day after we got home, we had to race back to Saint Francis when Harry's fever hit 101.5 that morning. Three days later, we went home again. This time, though, I was going to have to give Harry the IV antibiotic through the PICC line, flush the PICC catheters every day, and change the PICC line bandage every couple days, yet another process requiring masks and gloves.

Journal entry - January 30, 2007

Everyone ends up at the Cross. One way or another. Either like Jesus or like His mother Mary who has to watch. I used to talk about marriage being a reflection of God's love. Sometimes I look at Harry and see the reflection of all my failings - the times I've been impatient or unsympathetic. Harry is my chance - as Aunt Eileen says, "This will be your biggest triumph."

Father, please help me to love Your will.

---

[1] Francis Fernandez, *In Conversation with God*, (London: New York: Scepter, 2003) Volume 1, page 281.

"We got married just in time."
- Harry

~ Back Home After Round Two ~

Sometime in our life, almost all of us end up on one side or the other of a skewed relationship. For some of us, it's when child and parent reverse roles. For others, it's when lovers become caretakers. It feels unbalanced, especially for a man who believes his role is to take care of his wife.

Over the months, Harry had watched me sweep dead skin off the bedroom floor each morning, change sweat-soaked sheets in the middle of the night, empty bedside commodes, clean up vomit and other bodily byproducts, flush out catheters, bandage PICC lines, and myriad other things neither of us would ever have imagined. There were times when he couldn't roll over without my help. Times when he couldn't get off the toilet without my help. This is part of the life of human beings, and with him being seven years older than I, we both knew going into the marriage that this time would probably come. That didn't make it any easier for him. Worst of all, sometimes when the poor man threw up or worse, he'd say weakly,

"Don't worry, I'll clean that up," eyes closed, still reeling.

I understood how he felt, but I had absolutely no idea how to fix it. So what happened after we got home from the second round of chemotherapy was a blessing in disguise. I still look at the scar on my toe and smile.

Harry was physically stronger after the second round of chemo than the first. When we got home this time, he did not need a walker, and he could use the toilet and take a shower with little difficulty. Fatigue was his main problem. So we spent a lot of days out on the deck and evenings reading in bed. Every evening, after reading for awhile, one of us always turned to the other and asked,

"Do you want some toast?"

That was my cue to go out to the kitchen in my pajamas, toast a couple of nice, thick pieces of bread, slather them with butter and strawberry jam, and bring them back to bed for us.

The night of this event was just like every other night since we'd been home. We were happily, companionably, luxuriously lounging in bed reading when Harry asked if I wanted toast. I said yes, kissed him on the cheek, got out of bed, and went into the kitchen in my bare feet. I put two slices of bread into the toaster. While the bread was toasting, I absentmindedly opened the refrigerator and took out a large, glass jar of jam. I didn't have a good grip, however, and suddenly the jar fell from my hands, smashed onto my big toe, and shattered. There was glass, jam, and a widening pool of blood everywhere. The gash on my toe was so long and deep that I could see the bone.

As I watched the jar fall, my first thought was,

"NOOOOOOOOOOOOOOOOOOOO!"

But as I looked down at all the glass and blood, I can't tell you how happy my heart suddenly was for Harry, and my very next thought was, "I clearly am in bad need of help, and Harry is the only one here to help me!"

Just then, Harry called out to me,

"Is everything okay?"

"Not really," I answered, "I need help. I think I might have broken my toe, and there's blood and glass everywhere."

Harry came slowly out of the bedroom and surveyed the situation. Without a word, he went back into the bedroom and reemerged with a pair of my flip-flops. He came over to me, bent down, and somehow managed to get one flip-flop on my good foot, and a wad of paper towels around the bleeding foot. Then he put my arm around his neck and helped me hobble around the glass and into our bedroom. He helped me down onto the bed and propped my bleeding foot up on the rail across the end of the bed. He went back to the kitchen, filled a large bowl with warm water, and then went into the bathroom for Neosporin and bandages. He came back into the bedroom, washed my feet, tweezed the glass out of my toe, applied the Neosporin, somehow fashioned a butterfly bandage, and bandaged my toe. Finally, he went back into the kitchen and mopped up the mess.

When he was finished in the kitchen, he came back to bed bearing more hot buttered toast, lay down beside me, happily pulled me over "in the pocket", and fed me pieces of toast with kisses in between.

At that moment, he *knew* he was Harry My Hero. I knew it all along.

We didn't add that story to the blog. It was just for us. I don't think Harry will mind that I told you, though.

The Daily Leamy Blog - Wednesday, January 31, 2006
Hello our dear LPCTC (Little-Prayer-Chain-That-Could),
We have now been home a week and are finally adjusting to being back
HOME. I found that for the first few days, I kept looking at the clock and

thinking about what they were doing on the 5th floor at St. Francis at that moment - even found myself missing our favorite night nurse. Touch of the Stockholm Syndrome. Anyway, we've finally started to feel like we're home again. We do still have a fox hole mentality, but it's a much nicer foxhole, and our socks are dry.

Harry was supposed to get a bone marrow biopsy on Tuesday, but his platelets weren't high enough yet. So he hopped off their exam table (ok, that might be a little exaggeration, but he was very convincingly spry), and we went to McDonald's and ate sausage biscuits in the morning sun. Heavenly. I've been giving him his daily IV dose of antibiotics and have become quite the little nurse. I can flush that IV, give him the meds, flush the line again and top it off with Heperin without even waking him up.

We continue to say the rosary every night and ask for Harry's complete healing, but also for the grace to keep plugging away at this. I don't know how we could have spent 28 days in the hospital and both come out so drained, but we did. Good thing God doesn't get tired.

We pray a prayer of thanks for each of you as well.

The Daily Leamy Blog - Friday, February 23, 2007
Stealing Home - from Eileen

We are finally rounding 3rd, and the home base coach is waving us in. This was a gorgeous day, and Harry Our Hero ate bacon and eggs this morning and spaghetti this evening. Life is good.

This week, our "bump" was a problem with the PICC line snaking through Harry's arm into his heart. This is the thing that we use to give antibiotics and fluids and that the nurse uses to draw blood cultures. It has 3 ends, but one was completely clogged off, and Harry's arm was turning a very unnatural, albeit lovely, shade of purple. This naturally happened at about 10 at night several nights ago, because one of the laws of medicine we've learned is that nothing happens while doctors are actually in their offices. Anyway, I called a 24 hr. nurse to discuss the situation, but Harry and I just kept looking at each other thinking exactly the same thing - "There's NO WAY we're going back to the hospital!" We even talked about ripping the thing out ourselves - that's how determined we were. The next day, another one of the 3 ends clogged up, and I was quite worried yesterday about a contingency plan for the weekend, when "out of the blue," a nurse from the infectious disease group, of all people, called and asked how things were going. Turns out she's one of their infusion nurses meaning she knows all about this PICC line/IV stuff. In about 15 minutes, she developed a couple of contingency plans that would see us through until Tuesday (when we see O'Rourke again). It was just as if God Himself called and said, "Don't worry. I've got your backs."

It's not lost on me, as you may have been thinking, too, that all this has happened and is now coming to the first plateau just as we enter Lent. I think about that Psalm, "Create in me a clean heart, Oh Lord." We're certainly all heading toward Easter with power-washed hearts, but I know in my case, at least, how shockingly easy it's been to fall just a little to the side and get distracted by some little, meaningless thing. Distracted from the beauty of what we've all seen happen to Harry. I guess this is one of the biggest challenges we face in this world. Staying focused.

Harry is sitting in his leather chair by a lovely fire. Last night he said we got married just in time. Now there's a man with a clean heart.

Love, love, love to you all.
Eileen

"Promise me we're never going back there."
- Harry

~ Bad News Again ~

On April 4, 2007, we once again packed up lamps, quilts, and Aerobed® and settled into Saint Francis for Harry's third round of chemotherapy. The rash Harry had developed was again alarming. Every morning when he awoke, he looked as though he were completely covered with flour. Harry's entire body was covered with a layer of white, dead skin continually sloughing off, so the doctors doubled the dose of steroids he was getting to try to contain it. The result was that Harry barely slept and developed a frightening dementia of which he was painfully aware. For the previous two treatments, since we lived nearly an hour from Saint Francis, we had remained in the hospital until Harry's white cell counts were back up to normal just in case he developed any problems. This time, even though Harry's white cell counts were still very low, the doctors persuaded us that he was much less likely to develop an infection at home than in the bacteria infested hospital, so they released him on Friday, April 20. This was always the thing I feared most. That he would be at home on my watch and suddenly be overcome with infection, and I wouldn't be able to get him back to the hospital in time. I was truly terrified to take him home, but I also knew how hard it was on him to be in the hospital, so I reluctantly agreed. I packed up our room, the nurses and I loaded Harry into the Green Bubble, and we went back home.

The very next morning, my worst fears came to pass. Harry woke with a fever of 104 degrees. He was weak and vomiting and increasingly disoriented. I speed dialed Dr. O'Rourke's office, and they told me to get Harry back to Saint Francis immediately. I ran back to the bedroom and tried to help him out of bed, so we could get to the car, but he was too weak to stand. I didn't know what to do, and in a panic, ran out the back, stood in our driveway, and screamed,

"STEEEEVE!"

at the top of my lungs. Steve suddenly appeared on his deck as if by magic. All I could do was scream,

"HELP!"

and Steve came running down the hill. As the two of us ran back into the house, I told Steve what was happening and that we had to get Harry into the car. Between the two of us, we managed to get Harry's arms around our shoulders and half drag him to the car. I drove like a bandit back to Saint Francis, silently pleading with God while Harry slumped and moaned next to me. When we got to Saint Francis, they were waiting for us at the Emergency Room entrance. They lifted Harry out of the car, put him on a gurney, and took him directly to the ICU. With the infusion of intravenous antibiotics and fluids, however, he improved almost moment to moment, and by the time Dr. O'Rourke's partner, Dr. Spector, got there, his fever was down to 99.4, and he was asking for something to eat. By the next day, he asked me to go to Starbucks and get him coffee and a scone. He had cheated death one more time.

Three weeks later, we left Saint Francis once again. For the rest of May and June, Harry's strength started to return and the "chemo-brain" fog started to dissipate. Harry's nephew was getting married in Aspen, Colorado on July 7, and all Harry's brothers would be there.

Harry badly wanted to go, and we decided the benefits of his seeing his family outweighed the travel risks. He needed to do this very normal thing. So we flew to Denver on Thursday, July 5 and then drove to Aspen the next day. We thought driving from Denver to Aspen might help Harry's body adjust to the altitude more gradually than if we flew directly into Aspen. Friday night, Harry was able to put on his game face for his family, and we all went to the rehearsal dinner in town. In spite of our efforts, however, Harry was exhausted and dehydrated by the altitude. He spent the morning resting in our hotel room, but he rallied in the afternoon and walked around the town with everyone Friday afternoon. He even managed to stop and surreptitiously buy me a singing birthday card.

The wedding was at a lovely ranch up in the hills outside of Aspen, and no one was aware that Harry was having any difficulty. Back in our room, however, he headed straight for bed. We both longed for lower ground.

Monday, July 9, was my birthday. We had a lovely, relaxed drive back to Denver, and on the way, we were amazed to see a huge statue of Jesus on a hill off in the distance. We went to investigate and found the 22 foot statue, sitting on an 11 foot base, on a hill at the Mother Cabrini Shrine about 15 miles outside Denver. We were the only people at the shrine, and we walked the peaceful Meditation Walk and then said a rosary in the Rosary Garden. This was the calming antidote we needed to all the frenzy and activity we had just been through. We both breathed more deeply, smiled more serenely. That night, I wrote in my journal:

July 9, 2007 - My Birthday

Harry and I discovered the Mother Cabrini Shrine outside Denver. Beautiful gardens with her wisdom etched in stone. "Love, and God will take care of the rest." "Without cost, you have received. Without cost, you have to give."

What a birthday kiss from Heaven!

Once we got back home, Harry seemed to plateau. I kept after him about eating and the need to drink eight bottles of water, but he kept saying,

"Let me have control over my own health. What I need from you is for you to love me."

I prayed for God to help me be still and do this Harry's way, but it was a struggle, and I wrestled with myself daily. We talked about this struggle and about how hard it was for me to sit and say nothing, but Harry was adamant.

"I don't need you to monitor me. I need you to love me."

We continued to pray the rosary every day and to offer up all that happened in our daily lives. I offered the terrible struggle I was having. It was a kind of suffering the Blessed Mother knew all too well. The suffering of the helpless witness.

It was hard to trust Harry to do what he needed to do, but I realized the one I was really having trouble trusting was God. I wanted so badly to want whatever God's will was, but I was terrified of the pain to come. Every day, I prayed,

"Help me want Your will. I'm so afraid of what that is."

Harry never expressed any of these fears. Through the summer, he continued to go to O'Rourke's office once a week for blood work. Sometimes he needed platelets, sometimes a unit or two of blood. This became normal life, and Harry rarely seemed anxious. His mood continued as arrow straight as always, and I was amazed at how good he was at staying in the day. He was still trying to tend to his childrens' needs, starting each day with reassuring phone calls to each of them, especially to John and Jennifer. These conversations were taxing for him. It didn't help to start each day reminded of his plight, yet he continued, putting their needs before his.

In mid-September, Harry once again developed a fever which we knew was likely indicative of another infection. This time we didn't wait for Harry to get worse. I gave him some Tylenol and called O'Rourke's office right away, and they once again sent us to Saint Francis. This was not the frantic kind of trip we had made the last time. Harry was strong and clearheaded, and could walk to the car perfectly with no trouble. Through the summer, Dr. O'Rourke had been talking about a fourth round of chemotherapy in the fall, anyway, so we thought we might very well be at Saint Francis for the long haul. I routinely left the Aerobed® in The Green Bubble, so we just got into the car and drove off as casually as if we were heading to the grocery store.

When we got to Saint Francis, they immediately hooked Harry up to an IV and started giving him fluids and antibiotics. As always, his fever started to go down, and everything proceeded in what we now considered a routine manner.

Early the morning after Harry was admitted, Dr. O'Rourke came into his room. We greeted him like an old war buddy, but he looked uncharacteristically somber. He sat in a chair at the end of the bed, looked at Harry and said,

"We got the results of your blood work from last week. The leukemia has returned with a vengeance. There is nothing we can do anymore. Another round of chemo won't do any good. You need to go home and get your affairs in order. You have maybe 3-6 weeks."

Harry and I were completely dumbstruck. We went numb. We stared at O'Rourke who himself sat staring back at Harry. No battery of questions would change this. There wasn't anything to say.

Still looking straight at Harry, Dr. O'Rourke got up, shook Harry's hand, and said,

"Good-bye."

My brave Harry gave him a smile and said,

"Thanks for everything, Mark."

Less than an hour later, we were back in The Green Bubble, silently heading home. When we got home, we went straight out to the deck where Harry sat down to have a cigar. As Harry sat smoking and looking out over the lake he loved so, he finally spoke.

"Promise me we're never going back there."

"What if you spike another fever?"

"No matter what, we're never going back there. Promise."

I promised.

"Jesus wept."
- John 11:35

～ God Shows His Heart ～

Our native tongue is tears. Our tears speak right to God's heart.

I have not shown you all the anguish, all the pathos Harry and I endured. Looking at it all piled here in a heap might tempt you to think this is a tragic story. Trust me when I tell you it is not. I know. I live it still.

God came to us on a cross. It was not nails that kept Christ on the Cross. It was love. Jesus joined love with suffering on the Cross and made them one. But what is love? In the Douay-Rheims translation of the Bible, Saint Jerome translated "love" as "charity". Love as action, not just feeling. The Cross is God's love in action. We come back to God carrying our own cross and thanking Him for allowing it. God loves that. Loves for us to be thankful for everything without picking and choosing, without sorting into "good" and "bad" piles. We think there are two piles, but God thinks there is only one. It's all the same. It's all love.

God thinks this is a good story. Who am I to tell Him He's wrong?

So I'll tell you just one moment, maybe the most profound, transforming moment of my life. I'll tell you the moment God showed us His heart.

After O'Rourke's death knell, Harry and I were in shock. Shock is a wonderful shield. Shock let us take a machete slash to the head and still hug the nurses good-bye. Shock wound gauze around the gashes, so we could get in our car and drive all the way back home. But after we'd been home for awhile, after we'd gone to bed, shock wore off, and there was nothing left to do but bleed. We started convulsing, howling, hemorrhaging. My head was on Harry's shoulder, my arm across his chest, but I couldn't feel him. All I felt was the inferno of my nerves exploding, firing off flares. I saw Harry sobbing, but all I could hear was a gusting squall screaming through the blown-open hole in my heart. We could not speak, could not pray for help. All I could manage was a flicker of a heartbeat toward God.

That was all God needed. In that instant, I tell you truly, I could feel God crying. He was not just looking on with sadness, compassionate but removed. He was right there sobbing with us. Washing us with His tears. When I saw that, an astounding thing happened. I was immediately transfused with both joy and sorrow. Transported by joy at feeling God so close, the most profound joy I have ever experienced till then or since. But I was also suffused with sorrow. Sorrow at God's anguish. Sorrow for my own ingratitude. I was suddenly bursting, gushing with love for God. All I wanted was to ease His sorrow. To do something to show Him how grateful we were.

It was then I realized Harry had stopped sobbing as well. Without moving, I whispered,

"Do you feel that?"

"I do."

"What does it feel like to you?"

"It feels like God is crying."

Yes.

God's tears were having the same soothing effect on both of us. It was crazy, the tenderness washing over us. Our hearts were brimming not just with love for each other, but with love for God. Our very own God. Now you may say we were just projecting our feelings onto God. I accept that. You might be right, but here is what I know. What happened was a complete surprise. I had never experienced anything like it before. The idea that "...Emmanu-él ('God with us') "[1] meant God was right there in the thick of things was completely outside the scope of my imagination. I had always seen God as standing outside my suffering, helping, but not participating. I know, too, that Harry and I had the same experience at the same time. God was not just supporting us, God was *with* us, all three of us with our arms around each other. God spoke right to our hearts in tears, and the message was,

"We are in this together. I'm in this with you."

Most important of all, this experience profoundly altered our actions. We wanted to console God. We wanted to show Him, not just tell Him, how grateful we were.

Luckily, God had a plan for that, too.

1 Matthew 1:23

"You are my anchor and my compass."
- Harry

~ Harry Has His Say ~

Harry was a family man. He reveled in family. When his children were young, and he was driving them thither and yon, if he saw another van full of kids, Harry would slow down and give the other parents a little salute as they passed by.

"I think they thought I was crazy, but I loved the camaraderie of us out there working our butts off for these families."

When Harry's daughter, Jennifer, commented that he, "...got such a tough break," in life, Harry shook his head and answered,

"Not really. I got to have two families full of kids. Lots of people love me. It could be a lot worse."

Harry tended those two families for nearly all of his adult life. When he was fit and robust, he spent his physical stamina on his kids. When he was sick, he spent his mental stamina still being "Pop" for all our children, still being the reassuring voice they needed to hear. And he spent his spiritual stamina "offering it up." I have come to believe that just as God wants us to be good stewards of the time He gives us, of the talents He gives us, and of the treasure He gives us, He also wants us to be good stewards of the suffering He allows us so that none of it ever goes unused. Unburnished. So every time we prayed, Harry and I offered our suffering for our children and for our brothers and sisters.

Dr. O'Rourke had told Harry to go home and put his affairs in order. Harry's financial affairs were already in order, but there were some affairs of the heart that he felt he could no longer put off. Harry had done everything a father could do and more. But now, at the end of his life, he wanted to do things his way, and he hoped his children loved him enough to understand and to honor his wishes. Wherever there is good, however, there is also evil inciting discord and division. We had seen this several times during Harry's illness, but a particularly divisive situation occurred shortly after we left the hospital. Harry's will was opened prematurely. Pandemonium ensued, and there was an emotional onslaught pressuring him to rewrite it. Harry was deeply disappointed, and he didn't feel he had the stamina to cope with all the fallout. Yet, he was still Harry, and he immediately forgave everyone involved. He didn't want anyone to get distracted from his purpose. He believed he had something far more important to talk about than money.

The day we returned home, we sat out on the deck and talked about what Harry wanted to accomplish. He knew it was going to be difficult, and he wanted to handle things just right. He wanted a plan. So we decided it would be most helpful for him to talk to our priest, Father Miles. I bypassed the parish office and called Father Miles directly on his cell phone. He said he'd be happy to come out the next afternoon.

Father Miles arrived about one in the afternoon on Wednesday, September 12. Neither Harry nor I knew the significance of that particular day, and if Father Miles did, I do not recall him saying anything about it. Now, telling you this story, I discover that September 12 is the feast day of The Most Holy Name of Mary. Mary wafted everywhere throughout our lives. Yours, too. Mary, our warrior mother, in blue robes and combat boots. Harry was already sitting out on the deck in his robe and slippers, a blanket over his legs and a cigar in his mouth. Father Miles and I walked out on the deck, and Harry immediately offered Father a cigar. To my surprise, Father Miles happily accepted. Harry wanted me to stay and talk with him and Father to help explain things, so I started by telling Father about the fiasco with Harry's will. Harry went on to explain that what he wanted to talk to his children about was already going to be hard, and now all this clamor over his will was making it even harder.

What Harry wanted to explain, what he wanted his children to finally accept, was that he wanted to die with just me there. He wanted to die alone in my arms. When their mother died, there had been a long death watch, their house crowded with people waiting. Harry most emphatically did not want that. He felt that throughout all the hospital stays, all the trauma, he had stayed true to our plan to let our love flow out and take care of everyone else. His death was different, though. He was going to die the way he wanted.

I thought that was my cue, so I excused myself and went back into the house, so that Harry could talk with Father Miles privately. Every now and then, I looked outside and saw that Harry was doing most of the talking while Father Miles listened and nodded. This seemed like a good sign. At least he was getting everything off his chest.

After a couple hours, Father Miles came in and said they were finished and he was leaving. He and I went back out to the deck to say good-bye, and I could see that Harry was calmer and more at peace. They had talked the situation over, and they had a plan. Harry was going to call all of his children and ask them to come to the lake on Saturday, so that he could talk to them all together. Father Miles was going to be there as well to start things off with a prayer and a few observations of his own, and then Harry was going to make some general comments that applied to all of them. After that, Harry was going to go out on the deck and have each one come out and talk to him alone. I suspected, as you might, too, that this was not going to go over well. But I also believed, as I hope you do too, that it didn't matter what anyone else thought of how Harry handled the situation. This was Harry's plan, Harry's life. Harry, who had for so long felt he had no control over any part of his life, needed to have some control over how he left this world. Harry needed to have his say.

Wednesday night, Harry called each of his children, and they all agreed to come to the lake. Larry and Donna were going to drive Jill down from Charlotte, so they would be there as well. After all the calls were made, we sat on the deck looking at the stars, and I asked Harry what he wanted me to do. His answer was swift and unequivocal.

"I want you to keep all these kids together. I want these kids to love you the way I love you. They don't understand how much they're going to need you."

The Daily Leamy Blog - Thursday, September 13, 2007
Dear hearts,

Yesterday was a very tiring day for Harry, but it ended on a calming note with him and Father Miles sitting on the deck smoking cigars together. Harry had a long conversation with Father in which he was able to say some things in confidence to an outside observer he trusts and get some good advice and comfort.

Today, he slept a lot of the day, and then sat on the deck and read, and - you guessed it - smoked a cigar. Everything is taxing and requires him to spend some of the finite energy he has left. Today it's hard to get a smile out of him. He can pull himself together long enough to have a short phone conversation,

211

but he's always exhausted afterward and always aware of what's happening to him. Last night, as we were slowly walking back in from the deck, him leaning on his cane on one side and me on the other, he said, "Looks like this leukemia thing is really going to happen." But the night before last, as we prayed the rosary, he prayed that he be cured. Still practicing the virtue of hope.

I asked him last night what he wants me to do, and the first thing he said was, "Keep all these kids together." Since the day we were married, his and my hope has been to meld (old midwestern card playing term) a family out of these two families. Even at this end point of his life, he carries this in his heart as his overriding wish.

You are all in our prayers as we know we are in yours. Hard as this has been, we will each carry this profound experience every day in our souls.

Love,
Eileen

On Saturday, September 15, 2007, Larry, Donna, John, Jennifer, Jill and Phaedra all arrived (Jessamin was not able to make the long trip from Phoenix, but was in complete sympathy with Harry's purpose). Father Miles had arrived earlier and was sitting in one leather chair while Harry sat in the other one beside him. Father opened with a prayer and then talked about the importance of family and the importance of love. He then excused himself and left, and Harry had the floor.

Harry started by addressing the immediate problem that had been swirling for several days. He handled it the way he'd said he and I should handle our problems. He ran to it and addressed it head on. He was not discussing, he was telling. His words were direct, but his voice was tender.

"First, I want all this talk about my will to stop immediately. I don't want to hear one more word about it. I'm not dead yet, and the will is not what's important right now. Love and family are what's important."

My heart broke for him having to even address such a problem, but he was loving and kind, a dying man pleading with the people he loved to look where he was looking, see what he was seeing.

He talked about how much God had done for us all and how blessed we all had been. He talked about what he had tried to do through the years as their father, what he had tried to teach them. He talked about the importance of loving each other, supporting each other, and banding together. He talked about how he had tried to support each of them all the while he was going through his ordeal. He tried as gently yet firmly as he could to tell them that he loved them all, but that since it looked like this may be the end, he wanted to spend what little time he had left alone with me here at the lake, and that when the time came, he wanted to die in my arms, ending with,

"I know this is hard, but I hope you will understand and respect my wishes."

He then said he was going to go sit out on the deck and talk with each of them separately. Say good-bye, really, to each one alone.

Do you see? At this point, at this final moment, Harry was all about love. In the face of death, life became very simple. Harry thought he could spell it out for them. First he had tried to show them, and now he was trying to tell them. Love each other. Take care of each other. Love Eileen. Love Phaedra. Hold onto each other. And to drive his point home, he was playing the only trump card he had. Promise me. I'm a dying man. Say you promise.

I won't tell you what happened from there. It doesn't matter. All that matters is that Harry was an apostle. An apostle preaching love.

The next day, everyone had left but John. Things had settled down since the day before. John had clearly taken Harry's words to heart, and the three of us had a really lovely evening.

The Daily Leamy Blog - Sunday, September 16, 2007
Hello dear hearts,

Today may have been the most perfect day ever on the planet. Gorgeous weather, sunset boat ride, and Chicago style pizza (shipped from Chicago compliments of John and Em) for dinner. Harry continues to gain strength, increase in appetite, and pray for a cure with a clean and tender heart.

Last night, I was reading a meditation that said, "We lack faith. The day we practice this virtue, trusting in God and in His Mother, we will be daring and loyal. God, who is the same God as ever, will work miracles through our hands." So it's time to be daring and loyal - daring enough to claim Harry's life and loyal enough to trust. Toward that end, we are keeping our focus straight ahead and not doing anything that tries to niggle at our morale. Wonderful as you are and will continue to be, we're going to stop blogging for awhile at least, because it's too much a reminder right now. I know you understand.

We love you all dearly and count on your continued prayers. No more pussy-footing around.

Love,
Eileen and Harry

Everyone was gone, and we were in it by ourselves now. As we sat on the deck wordlessly watching the moonlight on the water and listening to the night sounds, Harry took my hand. He had one more matter of the heart he needed to say. Without looking at me, he said,

"You are so much more than I expected. You're both my anchor and my compass. Every day with you has been a treat."

It had been a long day, and we hadn't had a chance yet to pray a rosary. I asked him whether he felt up to it, and he said,

"Absolutely."

So we sat in the dark praying a rosary, offering up everything we had for our children and for our family. In spite of O'Rourke's dire predictions, we prayed for Harry to be healed. When we finished, Harry sat for a moment, just thinking, smoking his cigar, and finally said,

"You know if I get better now, there'll be no question who did it. It'll be all God.

"I felt something happen."
- Harry

~ We Pray ~

The Monday after everyone left, Harry and I were completely drained. It seemed all over but the waiting. Waiting for the inevitable. I'd been trying so hard to want God's will, discern God's will, and we ended every prayer, every request with, "If it is Your will." But now we were completely backed up against a wall. Given up on. I went into the bathroom and sat on the floor and sobbed. Slowly, though, something hard and resolute started to build within me. Conviction. Conviction that we had not been bold enough. Brave enough. I remembered reading that Pope John Paul II had said that before he really understood what God wanted us to do in prayer, he hadn't asked for enough. Now that he understood God's intention, he "...asked for *much*." We had not asked for enough.

Since Harry and I had come home from the hospital, our dear friends, Dave and Evie, had been bringing the Eucharist to us almost every day. The last time they were there, Evie told me,

"I know what the doctors said, and there's no question Harry looks awful, but I just have an overpowering feeling he's not going to die. This isn't his time yet."

So I went and got the phone, sat down on the bathroom floor, and called Evie.

"Evie, we have not been brazen enough. We have not been brave enough to ask for the full extent of what we want. I think it's time to be bold and ask God for an actual miracle. An out and out miracle."

My faithful friend, silent for just a beat, breathed a sigh of relief and said,

"Thank Heaven! It's about time! We'll be over tomorrow."

When I hung up the phone, I felt calm and resolute. We were taking action. We were taking the only possible action, the only plausible action. I went out into the bedroom and told Harry,

"Dave and Evie are coming over tomorrow, and we're going to hunker down and pray for a miracle. No more namby-pamby. Just boldly ask for an out and out miracle."
Harry just nodded.

On Tuesday, Dave and Evie came bearing the Eucharist. Then the four of us sat down at our dining room table, looking out at the sun sparkling on the water on that glorious, bluebird day. Harry sat in the middle with me on his left, Dave on his right, and Evie standing behind him. Dave and I each had one hand on one of Harry's arms and our other hand crossed behind Harry, clasping each other's arm. Evie had both her hands on Harry's shoulders. Evie started to pray whatever came into her head, wherever the Holy Spirit led her. While she prayed, I just kept silently repeating,

"Please heal him. Please heal him."

On Harry's right, Dave was doing the same. We prayed like that for several minutes until Evie finished. We all sat still. We didn't know how or when something would happen, but we felt we were now waiting for something completely different. Something that was coming. It was like Advent. We were waiting with hope. More than hope. Waiting with anticipation. We decided to keep praying like this every day until that something arrived.

Wednesday, Dave and Evie brought the Eucharist again, and we repeated our prayers. Thursday, they came again, and we followed the same pattern. Sometimes the prayer was mournful, sometimes lyrical and light.

Still we waited.

That Friday, Dave and Evie came for the fourth time. We resumed our same positions, me on Harry's left, Dave on his right, and Evie behind him. We began praying just as we had before. I had my hand on Harry's arm and was meditating on the mantra, "Heal him, heal him" when I felt a physical change in Harry's demeanor. A subtle yet distinct straightening of his shoulders, sitting more erect. Later, Dave said at that same moment, the image suddenly came into his head of liquid gold flowing through Harry's blood vessels giving off a luminous light. As Harry straightened up, Evie ended her prayer. We all sat quietly for a moment, and then Harry said,

"I felt something happen."

That was all he said, but his physical change was striking. Something had happened.

Dave, Evie, and I sat looking at Harry without speaking, until Harry finally asked,

"Shall we move out to the deck?"

The four of us went out, Evie and I walking down to the lake, and Dave and Harry staying up on the deck smoking cigars. After a bit, Evie and I came back up to the house and sat with the men on the deck.

Harry took a puff on his cigar and announced with a little lilt,

"I think I'd like to go put a rock in the wall."

"Give God the last word."
- Eileen

∼ The Rock Wall ∼

The people from hospice could not have been kinder. The first time they came, I was overwhelmed and terrified, and they helped calm me down. Harry was in bed weighing the pros and cons of eating a peanut butter sandwich. When he finally decided, "Yes," they said that was a good sign. So they set up a schedule for which days the nurse would come, which days the social worker would come, etc. We were set. True to their word, they came faithfully. Except Harry was starting to improve. We were now a little over three weeks into the Death's Door Diagnosis, but whenever hospice came, Harry was outside happily working away loading a wheelbarrow with rocks and moving them to the back of the house. The last time they visited, I had just come in from Harry's worksite where I'd taken him a tuna sandwich and mint iced tea. As I sat at the table with them, the social worker very kindly said,

"Eileen, you're the only one we're actually helping. Harry's always outside working on the rock wall. We don't think there's any need for us to keep coming here. We're going to tell O'Rourke we're dropping you from our schedule."

220

Well, I hesitate to say this too loudly, but Harry is definitely getting stronger all the time. Last week, our good, good friends, Dave and Evie, came over a couple of mornings for cigar smoking, rockwalling, and dessert eating (Evie has given up bringing us actual food and gone directly to desserts instead. What a fabulous woman!). Harry has a zen-like focus on the wall which we are told is the way that people manage to do well - by blocking out all the scary thoughts.

Jen came Saturday and she and her dad spent most of their time working on the wall, and the wall had the same mesmerizing, calming effect on Jen that it does on Harry. I really think there's a clinical trial in here that someone should get NIH to fund. Rock wall therapy. Picking a placebo could be tricky.

A few weeks ago I was feeling low and crying when it dawned on me, "We're all still praying for Harry to be healed, so when will we know he's cured, and it's time to STOP crying?" The answer was embarrassingly obvious. Stop crying now. There's plenty of time later. Stop crying and give God the last word.

Love,
Eileen

Harry conceived the idea of the rock wall in the spring of 2006. Every night after dinner, we would take a boat ride around the lake. Harry was especially taken with the many and varied pavilions and pergolas people had built by the water's edge. After several weeks, Harry declared,

"We need a water feature, Eileenie!"

So in the summer of 2006, Harry excavated a large area down by the water and had several tons of river rocks delivered. At the time of his original diagnosis in October, 2006, he had barely started moving rocks to the excavation site.

When Dave and Harry were sitting on our deck after we prayed, Harry, still in a very weakened condition, surveyed the site. Not only was there the rock wall to consider, he had also planned to build wooden steps leading from the house down to a pavilion on the water. All that was there at the moment was a huge hole and a mound of dirt. Harry worried that he was going to leave me with an enormous mess on my hands. He was still alive, and he was still taking care of me, so he decided he'd better get up and start working. His only goal was to get as much done as he could before he died.

So every morning, Harry went out to the wall and kept working, wending wheelbarrows of rocks down to the site, heaving bags of concrete, lifting rocks on and off the wall, etc. Little by little, he gained stamina and strength. His muscles developed and his appetite returned. It wasn't long before he was working sunup to sundown, sometimes even later. He had a purpose and a focus. He spent most of the day pondering where to put the next rock. Nothing more or less weighty than that. He was in his element, in his glory. Once when I took a sandwich down to him, he confessed with some concern,

"I feel guilty like I should be spending time with you instead of working on this wall."

That was music to my ears. Dying men don't usually have the dilemma of working too hard. I assured him that he was doing exactly what he should be doing - exactly what I wanted him to do. I wanted him to live. The wall was helping him do that.

The days continued on, one more hope-filled than the next. Sunny autumn days with Harry at the rock wall early every morning and me shuttling coffee, mint iced tea, sandwiches and cookies out to him throughout the day. Sometimes I sat outside and just watched. I didn't want to help him. We were in no hurry. I was afraid of what might happen if he *didn't* have the wall to work on, so I didn't want to speed things up.

Harry's skin had stopped the terrible shedding, but was still paper thin. Sometimes he would come into the house with a huge wound, skin scraped off from his elbow to his wrist. When we came home from the first round of chemotherapy, O'Rourke had told Harry not to even try any gardening because he was too susceptible to germs and bacteria from the soil. Now here Harry was with his skin all scraped off and his arms bleeding. I was terrified he was going to get an infection that would be the thing that killed him. Harry was not fazed, however. He'd always just have me clean the wound and spray a liquid bandage over it to protect it. After awhile, there had been so many of these episodes with nothing happening, Harry felt comfortable even going into the lake. There were many days when Harry was working outside while I went for a run. When I came back, I would go down to the lake, and Harry and I would cool off, bobbing and noodling around, talking and laughing, just loving the lake and each other.

Winter passed and the beautiful mountain laurel, native rhododendron and dogwood started blooming. Breathing the clean mountain air, working in the sun, Harry grew stronger, more resilient, finally one day, looking out at the lake and announcing,

"I want to make a pilgrimage."

∼ Pilgrimage ∼

Where there is good, there is always evil, and where there is evil, good. Whenever we are trying to be our best selves, the forces of evil are there trying to thwart us. They work all the harder the closer we come to God.

Harry wanted to take a very particular kind of trip. A pilgrimage is not just a trip, it's a journey. It is a journey to a sacred site in supplication for supernatural aid, in thanksgiving for help already given, or in obedience to a religious obligation. A pilgrimage is considered all the more worthy when the pilgrim endures some hardship along the way. Fortunately for Harry, I supplied plenty of hardship. It helps me now to tell myself that.

Harry knew exactly where he wanted to go. He wanted to make a pilgrimage to the Basilica of the National Shrine of the Immaculate Conception in Washington, D.C., a nine-hour drive from our lake house. The Basilica is the largest Catholic Church in North America, tenth largest in the world, and is referred to as *America's Catholic Church*. The bishops in the United States designated the Basilica as a National Sanctuary of Prayer and Pilgrimage. In the Catholic world, it's a very big deal. Harry and I had never once spoken of the Basilica or any

224

other pilgrimage site, but somehow he knew about it, and that's where he wanted to go.

We decided to leave as soon as possible. We spent the day after Harry's declaration doing laundry and packing. Harry made his customary travel "gorp" - five pounds of peanuts, five pounds of M&M's, and five pounds of raisins, all mixed together for us to eat in the car. We planned to drive the entire distance in one day, and when we set out early the next morning, we were confident we hadn't forgotten anything.

We were wrong. We forgot to pray for protection.

Harry and I had a very easy relationship. True to our word in Jennifer's apartment after The Big Smack, we never fought. Whatever little idiosyncrasies we each had, the other found either completely charming or at least easy to ignore. We had just come through a year of living literally side by side in cramped hospital rooms and were more in love than when we'd married. We were the love of each other's lives. But if Harry was my hero, I was his Kryptonite. I was his only weakness. He told me once,

"You're the only person in the world who can hurt me."

I was the perfect point of attack to derail his pilgrim's progress.

The forces of evil cannot make us do anything without our consent. Our free will is the battleground. We are willing accomplices, however obliviously. Evil can be perniciously persuasive. Harry and I were barely an hour from home when it started. Quite suddenly, I was annoyed with everything about the way Harry was driving, and, much to our mutual surprise, told him so. He was driving too fast, driving too slow, too close to the center line, too close to the car in front. I gave him every benefit of my superior skills. I didn't see what was happening yet, and I was appalled at my behavior, but I couldn't seem to keep from criticizing. Heading up I-26 toward North Carolina, Harry decided it might help to travel through the fall foliage in the mountains, so outside of Asheville, North Carolina, he turned onto the scenic Blue Ridge Parkway. For a few blissful moments, I quieted down, and peace reigned once more, but it wasn't long before I started to get angry at having to crawl along at 35 mph around the winding mountain roads. I was now confused and alarmed by my hotheaded outbursts and lack of control, but I blundered on anyway.

Ever the problem solver, Harry concluded I must have low blood sugar. I hadn't eaten that morning, so it was a plausible and charitable explanation. He pulled up at a K&W Cafeteria, and we went in. The line was long, the room was hot, the food was greasy, and the tea was watery. The booths were all full, so we had to find a table. The table was dirty, and my chair was wobbly. All of this I communicated to Harry in an increasingly haughty harangue. To Harry's saintly credit, he uttered not a word in response to any of my outbursts. But as we headed back to The Green Bubble, I was rapidly turning into "Shrew wife" right before his eyes, and he finally faltered, asking in a flat tone,

"Should we just turn around and go back home?"

It was then that I finally felt the full weight of what was at stake. It was then that I realized what I was doing, and that if this pilgrimage was under such a ferocious attack, it was the very thing we must rush to do. All I could say was,

"I'm so incredibly sorry for how I've been acting. Please, please forgive me. All I know is we should get in the car and drive to the Basilica as fast as we can. Please try to ignore me until we get there."

With that, we got back into the car and drove pellmell to D.C., Harry focused and resolute, and me silently praying, "Please help me. Please help me. Please help me." Still, at one point while I was driving, I was so angered by the voice on the GPS that when Harry tried to calm me down, I snapped, "This is between me and her!" Dementedwife.

When we finally got to Washington, it was 4:45 in the afternoon. We discovered there was an evening Mass starting at 5:00. We parked the car and ran into the church just in the nick of time. At Mass, the holiness of the shrine, the words of the Scripture readings, and the wonderful homily all had a calming, uplifting effect. At the end of Mass, we walked with the other pilgrims out of the church, turned and looked at each other, fell into each other's arms, and clung together crying.

We spent the entire next day in the Basilica praying in every one of its 70 beautiful chapels and going to Mass at noon and again at five.

We drove back home with my arm through Harry's arm and my head on his shoulder. We had learned a powerful lesson. During the past year, we had seen this same kind of attack in the alternately lowly or lofty actions of those around us. All we knew was that if there was evil at work, it meant there was good at work, too. We must be doing something right. As Harry concluded,

"Maybe we're making progress."

Harry praying for the Blessed Mother at the Basilica.

"Whatever you did for one of these...you did for me."
- Matthew 25:40

Thank You Notes

How do you write God a thank you note? What do you get Him for a gift? The genius of God is we never have to wonder. He already has a wish list, and there's only one thing on it.

In the coming months, Harry's teeth started to break off in his mouth, a side effect of the chemotherapy. He didn't even have to be chewing something. He could swallow, and that little pressure from his tongue would break a tooth in half. As with everything else, Harry took this new development in stride without complaint. However, our dentist finally sent him to an oral surgeon to have all his teeth taken out.

It took a couple hours for the surgeon to pull all Harry's teeth and for Harry to recover from the anesthesia. The surgeon packed Harry's gums with gauze and gave him a dose of pain medication to get him through the long drive back to the lake house. Since we lived so far from civilization, before we started for home, we decided to stop and get Harry's antibiotic and pain prescriptions filled. So we stopped at Walmart, and I assured Harry that I would just run in, get the prescriptions filled, and be right back while he dozed in the car. That was my honest intention. But the pharmacist was a little backed up, so while I waited, I wandered the store, amassing a cartload of things of which we had no need. I was ambling among the kitchenwares when my sweet loveperson suddenly rounded the corner, admonishing,

"Eileenie, you're getting distracted by shiny things!"

He was right. I had no defense. We went back to the pharmacy, picked up his prescriptions, and headed to the checkout line at the front of the store.

At the checkout, the young cashier (whose name tag identified her as Shirlee) was talking heatedly with her equally young husband who was holding a baby no more than six months old. They were trying to figure out how to make a credit card payment due by the end of that day when they had no money. Their tense conversation ended, and Shirlee started to scan our embarrassingly discretionary purchases. DVDs, books, potholders... . Nothing anyone needed. I asked her about their situation, and as she bagged our purchases, she confided that her husband had lost his job, she was the only one working right now, and they didn't even have money for diapers this week. Then she gave me a nervous smile and said, "Have a nice day."

When Harry and I got back to The Green Bubble, we just sat for a moment. We looked at each other, each struck with the same thought at the same time. These kids needed help. Just the money we had squandered on trivialities would have bought diapers for a month. So we decided to give them some help anonymously. The plan was for Harry to wait in the car and for me to run back into Walmart, *not* get distracted by shiny things, and put some money on a Walmart gift card for them. Then I would hightail it back out to the car, and we would make our getaway before Shirlee knew who did it.

I went back in, went to another cashier in a different department, put $100 on a Walmart gift card, wrote "God Loves You" on the outside of the little envelope, gave the envelope to Shirlee's manager, and asked him to give it to her. I watched from the doorway just long enough to make sure he gave it to her, and then I ran for the car. Harry and I were laughing and giddy as we drove away. Once we were home, we talked about what had happened, and I pointed out,

"Did you see that God presented this chance to us when you were suffering?"

"I did!" Harry nodded, smiling broadly.

"Then whenever you're going through something, we should look for whatever opportunity God is giving us to do something for Him."

Harry loved this. His eyes were just sparkling as he pushed it one step further.

"I was thinking of buying you diamond earrings," he said, seeing how far we were really going to go.

"Perfect! I don't need diamond earrings, so we can hang onto that money until God gives us another opportunity to do something with it."

Harry was beaming ear to ear. His mother's voice warning the child Harry not to let himself "get taken" was long gone. The love he told me that we were meant to share with our family to make their lives easier now reached beyond bloodlines. Now family meant God's family.

We made a pact that day that we would keep our eyes open for God's opportunities, especially at times when Harry was suffering.

Maybe we imagined it. Maybe God didn't really cry, but God did something that night. Something that forever turned our hearts. God provided several chances for us to do something for Him in the months to come, always related to Harry's suffering. And each time, no matter how much pain he was in, Harry would listen to me tell him the story of whatever situation had come up.

And his eyes would shine.

"I think I'm supposed to tell my story."
- Harry

∼ God Shows His Hand ∼

Which miracle should I tell first? The one Harry believed he was sup-posed to tell or the greater one? The cause or the effect? For God, mending the body is a breeze. Mending the will is a miracle.

Harry's body was growing stronger, but his knee was again filling with fluid from the staph infection. Dr. Jennings had already told us he would be willing to continue to drain the fluid from Harry's knee. All we had to do was call and say, "It's time," and Jennings would set it up. Harry put the procedure off as long as he could. He could toler-ate the pain, but his increasing inability to walk finally got bad enough that he couldn't work on the wall, and so we sounded the alarm, and Jennings scheduled the outpatient procedure for Tuesday, October 30. We were hoping Harry could just slide onto the operating table that morning, but the procedure was that he first had to come in the day before for routine pre-op. We protested, but the hospital pre-vailed, so on Monday, October 29, we left our lake haven and made the 45 minute drive to Greenville. We were still heading to Saint Fran-cis, but at least we were going to the Saint Francis Women's Hospital on the other end of town. Neutral ground. No one there knew us dur-ing our stay in the Winter Palace. But being back in any hospital envi-ronment had a numbing effect on us both. When we got to the hospi-

233

tal, we sat silently in the waiting room, shock starting to overtake us both. The pre-op nurse called us into a little room where there was a recliner for Harry to stretch out and elevate his leg. We were both so trembly that she ran to get blankets for us to try to warm us up and stop our teeth from chattering. The nurse was cheerily unaware of our situation and asked all the standard questions, but we were barely able to muster the answers between us. She chatted amiably as she tied the rubber tubing around Harry's arm to draw blood and easily found a vein. Unremarkable to her, but a little bit of a Godsend to us. She said they were going to do the blood analysis right then and there, so they would have the results before we left. As she untied the tourniquet, Harry came out of his stupor and managed in a weak monotone,

"Don't tell us the results."

That gave her pause, and she wasn't quite sure how to handle the situation.

"But we're required to tell you. That's our policy. You don't want to know your results?"

All we could muster was a mutual head shake. She finally agreed and got up and left. As soon as the door closed behind her, Harry and I both fell fast asleep. Forty-five minutes later, she returned, woke us up, and told us with a gentle smile that we could go home. The procedure was all set for 7:30 the next morning.

October 30 was blue and bright, crisp and cool, the sunrise kaleidoscoping across the lake. A good day to be alive. All we wanted, all we prayed for was that Harry's knee be restored and that we'd make it back home. A humble request. We were still in something of a stupor after our experience the day before, so even Harry slept late, and we barely got to the hospital in time. A nurse immediately started an IV on Harry, and they wheeled him into the operating room. Less than an hour later, Dr. Jennings came to tell me how the procedure went.

"Harry looks amazing compared to the last time I saw him," he said astounded.

"He's been out every day working on the rock wall."

"He's out lifting rocks?!" Jennings exclaimed, eyes wide with amazement.

"Every day. And bags of concrete."

Jennings was speechless.

"God's got him, " I said.

"Maybe so," Jennings smiled slowly, "Maybe so."

After a bit, the nurse came and told me I could go in and see Harry in the recovery room. I went in and found my hero wide awake, drinking juice, and chatting animatedly with the nurses. When Harry saw me, he grinned and said to the nurses,

"Here's my pumpkin flower!"

Lovely, but loopy. The nurses all smiled and said,

"He's been asking for you."

They said it would just be a few more minutes, and then he could get dressed. They left us alone, and Harry, still grinning, said,

"I have something to tell you."

"What?"

"I want to wait until we're out of here." Twinkly-eyed and beaming.

I ran to get the Green Bubble. A nurse wheeled Harry out, we hustled into the car, and peeled out of the parking lot.

"Okay, what did you want to tell me?" I asked, wondering if he had some drug induced revelation, but this is what he told me.

"I was lying on the operating table waiting for Jennings to show when the OR nurse came up with a clipboard in her hand. She looked at the paperwork and said, 'Well, everything looks good. All your blood work looks good.'"

He paused for effect. I played along.

"What do you mean?"

"Exactly what I asked, my loveperson. The nurse said, 'Your blood work all looks normal.'"

"Even your white cell count?" I asked suspiciously.

"Even my white cells."

"How about your platelets?"

"Platelets are normal."

I had to pull over.

If anywhere there exists a word more beautiful than "normal," it isn't in our language or any other language known to man.

Harry was normal.

But that wasn't all. Harry continued,

"When the nurse told me that, I just started telling her everything that had happened, how they sent me home to die, and how we prayed."

He stopped and thought for a minute. Then he looked at me and said,

"I think I'm supposed to tell my story."

That was the second miracle.

"For each of us, that we grow in wisdom and grace."
- Harry

~ Monday Night Prayers ~

The week after Dave, Evie, Harry and I prayed, the four of us felt that our work was done. Harry was so much better, we stopped praying for him and started thanking God instead. Monday night, we were all in a jubilant mood and got together again to play cribbage. We were having a relaxed, back-to-normal time, laughing, joking, teasing, and we all agreed we needed to make this a regular thing. So the next Monday evening, we got together again with the same lightheartedness to play cards. At the end of that evening, though, we looked at each other, and all had the same thought at the same time.

"Maybe God would like us to get together for something more meaningful than cribbage."

We believed that God had answered our prayer about Harry, and the realization started dawning on us that He wanted us to pray the same way, make the same impassioned plea, for other people. We knew without a doubt that God had given the four of us a rare friendship, and we now saw that He didn't just bring us together to get us through the leukemia. He wanted us to lift up others to Him as well. That night, we all decided we would start spending our Monday evenings together bringing all the prayer intentions we could gather to God.

The next Monday evening, we met to pray at Dave and Evie's home. I brought a little box of about a hundred small, fancy, note papers about the size of small Post-Its. Harry had put them in my Christmas stocking the year before, and I'd never been able to figure out what to do with them. Turns out they were perfect for prayer intentions. Evie found a small, wooden, treasure chest looking box, and we decided to write each of our prayer intentions and put them in the box. That first night, by the glow of a blessed candle that Evie lit next to an old family statue of the Blessed Mother, we each sat and wrote every intention that came into our heads. Our children, our brothers and sisters, this sick friend, that acquaintance in financial straits. We went around the table several times, each one reading his or her intention, and then all of us joining to lift it up to God. Harry prayed so sincerely, so movingly, he melted my heart. We went around the table until every intention was read, prayed, folded, and safely stored.

Each week, we brought new intentions to the table. Then when we'd finished praying each new intention, we emptied all the folded intentions onto the table and took turns pulling out papers and reading old petitions to pray for again. As weeks and months went by, our box became so full of folded papers with intentions, we'd pray as many as we could and then say a general prayer for all of them. As time went by, we began to see that sometimes when we randomly picked an intention out of the pile, it had been answered, so Evie found a pretty little gold, drawstring bag, and we began putting answered prayers into the gold bag.

Sometimes when we came to the table, one of the couples was low in spirits or one of us was especially fretful, but we discovered that by the end of the evening, we always felt we'd done some small thing for God, and He, in turn, had lifted our hearts and minds. All four of us came to value and guard our Monday evening prayer time even to the extent that if one couple was traveling, they still called the other couple on Monday evening and prayed over the phone together. Dave and Evie were emergency foster parents, and on occasion there were children in their home on Monday evening. We always asked the children if they would like to pray with us, and when they did, we asked them if they'd like to write any intentions for us to pray over and keep in the box. They wanted to join in every time, and so we all sat together, prayed together, and in the months to come we often pulled their heartbreaking intentions out and prayed for them once again. Sometimes Dave and Evie had out of town guests staying with them, and we always made them the same offer. I was often struck by the immediate intimacy of these sessions where strangers suddenly came together, cried together, and prayed together their most fervent fears. Harry's prayers were always the same. He prayed for our five children each by name. He prayed for his grandson. He prayed for his brothers and their conversions. He prayed for Dave and Evie and all their family. He prayed for an end to abortion and for forgiveness and healing for all those involved in abortion. He prayed for our country. He prayed for everything he could think of. But the prayer of his I love the most is a prayer I still have on the little slip of paper on which Harry wrote it. I give it to you here, so you can see it in Harry's very hand. I know he prays it still.

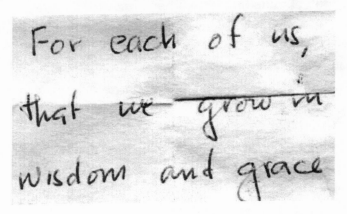

For each of us, that we grow in wisdom and grace

"I'm trying to consciously do good each day."
- Harry

∿ The Last Christmas ∿

Harry was an attentive gardener. Everything grew healthy and strong under his care. Sometimes he would say to me in a worried tone,

"Eileenie, who will take care of your flowers if I'm not here?"

Every spring and fall, we went to a local nursery and picked out plants for the yard and the large ceramic pots on the deck. Harry had a landscaping vision in mind for our entire lot from the front of the house down to the water in the back. He put in bulbs and bushes, planted petunias, pansies, lupine, and even trailing morning glories. In December of 2007, however, he had a different kind of landscaping in mind, and here are the seeds he planted.

One Monday night, after Dave, Evie, Harry, and I had finished our prayer session, Harry said he had been thinking about the upcoming Christmas. For the first Christmas since before we were married, four of our five children were coming home, and this time, Harry's grandson, Finn, would be there as well. Harry was not thinking about iPhones or digital cameras or any of the other technological toys that came out that year. He was thinking about one thing only.

Harry was thinking about Christ.

He was thinking about how to make Christ the center of this Christmas in a way our children could hear. He believed all our children needed to see the strength of his faith. He knew they had each fallen away from their faith, and he wanted to shepherd them back. He wanted to teach them, catechize them, through his example, but he wanted to do this in as gentle a way as possible. Harry also wanted a celebration befitting the birth of God among us and the miracle gift of his own life as well. He wanted everything to reflect thanks and praise.

The four of us talked for quite awhile, and then Evie remembered a tradition she and her brothers and sisters had started some years back when all their children were young. First, Evie and her sisters wrapped and numbered each of the figures from a nativity set. Then, they wrote out the story of Christ's birth and included the corresponding number for each nativity figure at the appropriate place in the story. On Christmas Eve, Evie's whole family gathered at one of their homes before going to midnight Mass. The Christmas creche stood empty on the mantel, and the wrapped figurines were all in a bag. Each child came up, took one of the packages out of the bag, then sat back down. One of Evie's brothers would read the story of Christ's birth, and when he came to a part where a number was indicated, the child holding the wrapped package with that number would unwrap the figurine and go and put it in the creche on the mantel. Harry immediately fastened onto this idea, believing that his three-year-old grandson, Finn, would give him the perfect passageway into our children's hearts and minds.

As Christmas grew closer, Harry became increasingly joyful. To our friends, Stu and Suzy, he e-mailed thanking them for a lovely fruitcake they had sent and bearing witness to the one he thought had spared him, saying,

Merry Christmas! I just did not want to let the opportunity go by without saying it.

As you know, I feel great. I attribute the disappearance of my leukemia to God, who heard our prayers. Thank you for the many that I know you said on my behalf. I now look at each day as a gift from God of the most miraculous thing, life. In gratitude, I am trying to consciously do good each day rather than simply avoiding sin.

Please be glad for your days and nights. Use them well. Know also, that I am praying for the two of you every day. I figure that I have a big prayer deficit that needs to be worked off and doing this is one way to do good.

Love,
Harry

Together, we began preparing the kind of celebration Harry wanted this Christmas to be. Since our marriage, we had been using a Renaissance style, papier mâché, nativity set that I had purchased years before. I thought it was lovely, but Harry never liked it. With his new-found fervor, I knew it was time for us to have a nativity set of our own, so I bought a brightly colored creche made by the South Carolina artist Jim Shore. The pieces were a simple folk art pattern painted with colorful, classic, quilt designs. When I brought it home, Harry and I unboxed all the figurines and set them on the mantel. Harry was delighted. He liked the simplicity of the figures and the way the set looked against the backdrop of the mountains and the lake through the windows. We set about wrapping all the figurines in tissue paper and putting them all in a basket.

Harry strung brightly colored lights outside on the deck and evergreen garlands tied with red bows on the second and third level banisters. We put beautiful, metallic angel figures playing harps and trumpets atop the kitchen cabinets. We strung the Christmas tree with strands of white angel lights. We bought the usual little stocking stuffer gag gifts and toys, and under the tree, we had lots of presents for little Finn to unwrap. Unlike years past, however, there was only one present, the same present in the same wrapping, for each of our children. We had sent the same present out to Phoenix for Jessamin as well. It was a present from Harry alone, and he wanted to be sure each of our five children had one.

I filled Christmas tins to overflowing with homemade batches of cookies and candy. Marshmallow fudge, white and dark chocolate peppermint bark, chocolate pecan drops, chocolate raisin drops, coconut chocolate drops, snickerdoodles, peanut butter blossoms with Hershey kisses in the middle, sugar cookies cut into shapes with my grandmother's cookie cutters for us to decorate, and pfeffernüsse like Harry's mother used to make. I baked pumpkin pie, cherry pie, pecan pie, and the mincemeat pie that only Harry (like my dad) enjoyed. And more cinnamon scones, as my dad would say, than you could shake a stick at.

Everyone arrived Christmas Eve day. Jennifer, John, Emily and Finn all flew in from New York, and we met them at the airport in Greenville, South Carolina. Jill and her husband, Chris, drove down from Monroe, North Carolina, and Phaedra drove down from Johnson City, Tennessee. There was lots of good natured greeting and hugging as everyone settled in. They had already arranged to have a community gift pile of presents to which they each contributed one wrapped gift and from which everyone would take one gift. So the pile of presents was mounting, plates of goodies were circulating, and the wine started flowing.

Harry and I had already decided that he would read the Christmas story first, and then we would all unwrap presents that night rather than on Christmas morning. So after awhile, Harry announced that he was going to read a story to Finn and explained how the nativity figurines were going to be handled. He and I had already decided that little Finn should have the honor of placing the baby Jesus in the manger, so we first gave that wrapped figurine to him. Then Harry took the basket, told everyone else to take out a wrapped figure, and went from one person to another until there were no more left. Things went quiet as people glanced surreptitiously at each other, more than a little perplexed, but everyone went along with the plan. Then Harry put down the basket, sat down on the couch with a pajama clad Finn on his lap, and began to read.

"2,000 years ago, the emperor of Rome ruled that everyone in the world had to register to be counted for a census. So a man named Joseph took his wife, Mary, far from their home in Nazareth to a place called Judea, to the town of Bethlehem to register. Mary was pregnant, and when they came to Bethlehem, Joseph looked everywhere for an inn where they could sleep, but the innkeeper told Joseph the only place in Bethlehem where they could stay was in a stable with the animals."

Harry stopped, and I unwrapped the first figures, a little sheep and donkey, and placed them on the mantel inside the creche.

"Joseph helped Mary to the stable and made her as comfortable as he could."

John bewilderedly unwrapped the second figure, Joseph, and put it on the mantle, while Emily unwrapped the third figure, Mary, and put it inside the creche.

"While they were in the stable, Mary gave birth to her baby, a son whom they named Jesus. She wrapped baby Jesus in swaddling clothes and laid him in the manger where the animals ate."

At this, Harry helped Finn unwrap the next figurine, the baby Jesus, and lifted Finn, so he could lay it gently in the manger.

"In that region, there were shepherds in the fields at night watching their sheep. And an angel of the Lord appeared to them, and the brightness of God lit up the night sky all around them."

Harry stopped, and Jennifer unwrapped the fifth figure, an angel, and put it on the mantel.

"The angel said to them, 'Be not afraid. I bring you good news of a great joy which will come to all the people; for to you is born this day a Savior who is Christ the Lord. And this will be a sign for you: you will find a babe wrapped in swaddling clothes and lying in a manger.' And suddenly there were hundreds of angels all singing, 'Glory to God in the highest, and on earth peace to men of good will.' And the shepherds said to each other, 'Let us go to Bethlehem and see this thing that has happened.' And they went and found Mary and Joseph and the baby Jesus lying in the manger."

Harry and a rapt Finn waited while Jill unwrapped the next package, the shepherds, and put them in the scene.

"The shepherds returned home, praising God for everything they had seen and heard. Then three wise men from the East came to Jerusalem, saying, 'Where is he who has been born king of the Jews? (They were talking about the baby Jesus.)? For we have seen his star in the East, and have come to worship him.'

When the king of Judea, King Herod, heard this, he was very troubled. So he had the three wise men brought to him in secret, and told them, 'Go and search for the baby and tell me when you find him, so that I may worship him, too.' So the three wise men went on their way, following the star which they had seen in the East, until the star shone from the sky over the place where the child Jesus was."

At this, Chris and Phaedra unwrapped the last of the packages, and put the figures of the three wise men on the mantel.

"When the wise men saw the star, they were filled with joy. They went in and found the baby Jesus with Mary and they knelt down and worshipped him. They gave him the gifts they had brought him, gold and frankincense and myrrh. When they were ready to go back home, an angel came to them in a dream and warned them not to say anything to King Herod, so they went back home a different way."

Everyone was quiet. Baffled. No one had any idea how to respond. They all waited for Harry to tell them what to do next. Harry kissed Finn on the forehead and said,

"The end."

He let that settle in for a moment and said,

"Now let's open our presents." He had one more stunner in store.

We all watched while Finn opened presents, and then everyone had a great time opening their presents out of the communal pile, making deals and trading when someone got something they wanted instead. There was lots of fun and merriment, and then we were down to the last presents, those mystery presents all identically shaped and wrapped. Harry handed one present to each of our children and our daughter-in-law, sat back down, and asked everyone to open them at the same time. More than a little perplexed and somewhat fearful, they each slowly unwrapped what Harry had given them. A hardback copy of Thomas Merton's classic, *New Seeds of Contemplation*. Harry was very drawn to Merton's idea that our true selves lived buried inside us, and that we needed to peel off the layers of culture and circumstance - what Harry termed 'the soup we're all swimming in' - and become the person God meant for us to be.

Harry let his gift sink in for a moment, and then he smiled and said,

"If you want to know what's going on in my head, read this."

Silence. Harry's focus on Christ was a lot for them to handle, and he knew it. But he looked peaceful, even somewhat radiant. He had done what he believed he was supposed to do. He knew he loved all our children, and he knew he wanted them to love each other and love God.

God showered us with gifts for Harry's last Christmas. God gave Harry the grace to finally, fully be the father God created him to be, feeding his family both body and soul.

The rest of us got the great grace of a glimpse of Harry's true self.

Harry transformed.

Harry transfigured.

"I continue to be amazed at God's goodness."
-Harry

~ Amputation ~

God is the king of second chances. Endless turns to set things right. Hindus call it karma. Christians call it the Cross. All our chances move us toward the Cross where God Himself sets everything right.

Harry loved our wedding anniversary. He firmly believed the occasion of our marriage was cause for special celebration. So for our fourth anniversary, he made all the arrangements to surprise me. He thought it was important for us to go someplace different and diverting where neither of us had ever been, so on January 17, 2008, we set out in The Green Bubble and drove to Charleston, South Carolina. Harry had reserved a suite at the charming Andrew Pinckney Inn in the historic district. The room was romantic and luxurious with a king-size bed, French doors leading onto a balcony, and a Jacuzzi. For the next two days, we ate scrumptious food, took carriage tours of the town, went to museums, and walked everywhere. First thing in the morning, Harry's knee was always swollen and achy, but he discovered that the more he walked, the better it felt, so we were hopeful that it wasn't too bad. We had a glorious trip, and Harry said that next year, we would go to Savannah. The night we got home from Charleston, Harry wrote to our friends Stu and Suzy.

Dear Suzy and Stu,

Eileen and I are just back home from a wedding anniversary trip to Charleston, SC. We had a wonderful time, in part thanks to your prayers! I continue to be amazed at God's goodness as He gives me day upon day in which to live and enjoy life. We are beginning to believe in the future enough to plan for it.

He was not just living, he was *alive*. Enjoying every day.

The second Sunday of February is celebrated as World Marriage Day in the Catholic Church. There is a special reception for all married couples, and couples married 5, 10, 15, 20 years, etc. are singled out and honored. Our friends, Dave and Evie, were the organizers for our parish, and I was excited to be attending this event for the first time. This was my "Vatican" marriage, the marriage inside the Church, and I was excited to be able to participate. So on Sunday, February 10, Harry and I gathered with about 50 other couples. There was lots of teasing and laughing and just generally having a good time. Harry and I had not yet been married a full 5 years, so they honored us with two Snickers bars for still being newlyweds and asked us to say a few words. Harry, true to what he saw as his new calling, got up and told his miraculous story. He was beautiful to watch, joyful and grateful, humble and heartfelt telling what God had done for him. Everyone was in tears, Harry included. Honestly, I felt honored to be his wife, to play any part in his story.

Every morning, Harry started the day by thanking God that he was still alive and that I was still alive. All our days are numbered, and Harry thanked God for each one individually. Then, he went outside to take up his work on the rock wall, and the work, in turn, sustained him, strengthening his body and spirit. He thanked God for the gift of the work and for the glorious place to do it in. On one of Phaedra's visits home, she introduced us to the Patty Griffin song, "Heavenly Day," which became Harry's anthem. He played it endlessly.

Oh, heavenly day
All the clouds blew away
Got no trouble today with anyone
The smile on your face, I live only to see
It's enough for me, baby, it's enough for me.
Oh, heavenly day, heavenly day, heavenly day

Tomorrow may rain with sorrow
Here's a little time we can borrow
Forget all our troubles in these moments so few
All we've got right now, the only thing we really have to do
Is have ourselves, a heavenly day
Lay here and watch the trees sway
Oh, can't see no other way, no way, no way
Heavenly day, heavenly day, heavenly day

No one at my shoulder bringing me fears
Got no clouds up above me bringing me tears
Got nothing to tell you, I've got nothing much to say
Only I'm glad to be here with you
On this heavenly, heavenly, heavenly, heavenly day

A lifetime ago, Harry's faith failed him completely, but now it lifted him daily. We continued to pray the rosary every day and to pray together every night. Not every prayer was the same. Some were, "Thank you," some were, "Help," and some were just showing God our hearts with no need for words. But we always prayed together. Harry also started reading the dense and daunting diary of Sister Faustina Kowalska, *Divine Mercy in My Soul* and sometimes read passages aloud to me. He was especially moved by one of the prayers from the diary, and we started praying this prayer at the end of each of our Monday night prayer sessions.

> *Eternal God, in whom mercy is endless and the treasury of compassion inexhaustible, look kindly upon us and increase Your mercy in us, that in difficult moments we might not despair nor become despondent, but with great confidence submit ourselves to Your holy will, which is Love and Mercy itself.*

In early spring, Harry had the idea of inviting all my family to the lake for a family reunion. I was absolutely thrilled. We ended up inviting over 60 family members for a three day visit over Father's Day weekend. Now we each had a project to focus on, and as I set about lining up lodging and planning meals for the reunion, Harry was pressing to get the rock wall and pavilion completed by June. One evening just as the sun was going down, Harry came into the house grinning and holding out his hand,

"I've got something to show you. You have to close your eyes."

So I closed my eyes and took his hand, and he carefully led me out the sliding glass doors, down the deck stairs, down the stairs leading to the pavilion, saying,

"Almost there. Just a few more steps..."

When we finally got down to the rock wall pavilion, Harry stopped, turned me around and said,

"Ok. You can open your eyes now."

I opened my eyes to the golden glow of hundreds of little lights strung all along the rock wall, over the pergola, and down the stairs to the water, twinkling all around us. Harry smiled and asked,

"Shall we dance?"

So we gently swayed in a sea of stars, Harry softly singing in my ear,

Just in time, I found you just in time
Before you came my time was running low.
I was lost, the losing dice were tossed,
My bridges all were crossed, nowhere to go

Now you're here, and now I know just where I'm going.
No more doubt or fear I found my way
For love came just in time, you found me just in time
And changed my lonely life that lucky day.

Our no swimming, no dancing prenup was officially null and void.

So life was going along in these heavenly days with happy work and lots to look forward to. One day, we were sitting on the deck talking about where in the backyard to put several long tables for a barbecue at the reunion when Harry's knee started to ooze. His knee had been increasingly swollen and achy again, and the tender skin was still so dry it actually cracked open, and fluid began to gush out. Harry pressed on the area that was swollen, and more fluid gushed out. Startled, I ran to get ointment, gauze and bandaging. When I got back, Harry said his knee felt quite a bit better. It certainly looked less swollen. So I cleaned it and dressed it, and we tried not to think about it.

The next day and the day after that, the same thing happened, so we called Dr. Jennings to set up what we believed would be a routine knee lavage just like Harry had had before. Jennings was able to get us in quickly, and we arranged to go to AnMed Medical Center in Anderson, South Carolina.

Since we were at a different hospital, the procedure this time was a little different from the other times. We arrived at the hospital the

253

night before, Harry was admitted, and they drew blood for blood tests. His knee was supposed to be cleaned out early the next morning. When morning came, however, no one came to prep him for surgery. Finally, Dr. Jennings came to our room with a look on his face that we recognized immediately. How is it possible to feel yourself go numb yet feel all the nerves in your body scream out as if they were being held to a fire? That's how I felt, and I wasn't surprised when Jennings finally said,

"The blood work shows that the AML is active again. We're going to put you on an IV antibiotic to try to help that knee infection, but we're not going to do the lavage."

Handshakes and thank-you-for-everythings. Nothing more to say. After some time, I can't even remember how long, I went out in the hallway and called my sister, Christie. I told her the news and asked her to call everyone and tell them the reunion was cancelled. Harry was devastated that the reunion was off. My dear loveperson was thinking about me and all the rest of us and didn't want to be the cause of our not having that time together. I just kept telling him it was all right. It didn't matter. Nothing mattered but him.

Harry stayed in the hospital another day while the IV antibiotics slowly seeped into his system. I stayed at home that night, wide awake all night staring at the ceiling, keenly aware of Harry not being there, of how it would feel forever without him there. I couldn't eat, couldn't sleep, couldn't talk, couldn't even cry.

Friday morning, I drove back to Anderson to bring Harry home. On the way there, I stopped for some bracing coffee and finally got up the courage to call my Aunt Eileen. She was always my lifeline, my calm port in a storm, but I hadn't been able to talk even to her till then. Just the sound of her voice had me choked up, and when she heard my voice, her own voice cracked as well. There was nothing to say, really.

I told her how even in the midst of this terrible time, my remarkable Harry was feeling badly about calling off our family reunion, and my aunt declared emphatically,

"We decided we're still coming. I'm an old woman, and I can't do much, but I can listen." At that, I finally let go and cried.

Journal entry - May 29, 2008

Spent the afternoon on the boat with Dave and Evie. Harry looked so bad. Evie talked "hypothetically" about what I would do "if anything happened to Harry." The tension and anger I feel are almost uncontrollable. That night, Harry and I had an awful discussion. It was so black and dark outside and inside our heads. I wanted him to just go ahead and tell me if he was throwing in the towel. Then I would, too. I'd stop frantically trying. We finally realized it might be just as simple as the fact he hadn't eaten and hadn't taken pain pills in time. He was behind the pain. He went out to smoke (about 11 p.m.), and I got in the car intending to drive to the North Carolina border - be "home" for just a minute. Turned on the radio, and it was playing a wonderful orchestral version of what Gram called the doxology. Over and over, louder and louder, grander with more and more instruments joining in. And in my heart, I sang with the music, again and again,

> *Praise God from whom all blessings flow*
> *Praise Him all creatures here below*
> *Praise Him above, ye Heavenly hosts,*
> *Praise Father, Son, and Holy Ghost.*

Indescribable joy. Lifted so high I was weightless. So I drove to the Citgo, bought Harry some Krispy Kreme doughnuts, and went back home.

Journal entry - June 3, 2008

Out walking and praying. Always start with the Divine Mercy Chaplet for Harry and for the conversion of all our five children. Then told God I was surrendering to His will. I know He created us, not the other way around, and His will is only and always good. This is very different from the beginning when I could not look at Him for fear of what His will might allow. So I was very calm, but also felt resigned if His will was for Harry to go to Him. I said, "Please just let us have a little hope, though," but then knew how absurd that was - to think God had taken away hope. God put this in my heart: "Now that you have surrendered to My will, you can be calm and give Harry the love he needs to heal. When you're afraid of my will, it takes all your energy. When you accept my will, your energy can go to loving Harry. My will IS your hope."

Journal entry - June 4, 2008

Driving, driving, down Highway 11. Passed a sign that said, "Thank God from whom all blessings flow." Turned around and went home.

Over Father's Day weekend, my Aunt Eileen, her son, Miles, and daughter-in-law, Cina, my sisters and their families, and my daughter, Phaedra and her friend, Matt, came to the lake. Terrible time though it was, I was glad to have them there for support. We did not spend the weekend crying. During the day, Harry marshaled all his strength and rallied. He was the consummate host, charming and funny as always. By this point, his knee was so bad that I was draining and dressing it every morning and every night, and the fluid oozing out was now green instead of clear. At one point, I told him,

"It doesn't matter that people are here. We should take you to the hospital."

Harry insisted on waiting, though, and every night, exhausted in bed, he'd earnestly ask me,

"Do you think everyone is having a good time?"

256

Harry had been worrying about me, and he knew how much my family meant to me. That's why he had suggested the reunion, and that's why he never once complained. It was an amazing show of love and selflessness that I still keep in my heart.

Monday morning, everyone had left, and Harry finally called Tom Fehring in Charlotte. Fehring told him to come to Charlotte immediately. We got in the car and were in Fehring's office by noon. He looked at the knee and told Harry that it had gangrene. To try to save Harry's leg, Fehring would first remove the prosthetic knee and clean out the knee cavity. Then we would wait and see whether the gangrene was gone. If it was, Fehring would put in another prosthetic sometime down the line. If not, he would have to amputate.

The idea of amputation was not new to us. During the second round of chemotherapy, the internists had talked with Harry about the difficulty they were having getting the knee infection under control. The only antibiotic that really controlled it was also the culprit that caused Harry's skin to shed resulting in more infection. Harry had told them,

"Amputate it. Let's just eliminate the problem."

At that time, the internists were stunned and said they thought there were still drug options they could try. Now I was silently wishing they had taken Harry's approach way back then, but it was too late now, and we were just relieved and grateful that Fehring was going to do anything at all. Tom left the room to arrange for Harry to be admitted for surgery, and we sat in the little examination room feeling the most hopeful we had felt in weeks. Help was here.

Unfortunately, we were distracted. We forgot about the time bomb ticking away in Harry's body.

That night, they started Harry on yet another IV antibiotic and took blood for tests. The next morning, Fehring came by and said he would remove the infected prosthetic later that morning. Hesitantly, I asked how Harry's blood work looked, and Fehring said it looked fine. Harry and I were both surprised and elated. We didn't want to ask any more questions. We didn't want to rock that boat.

After the titanium knee was removed that afternoon, we started the wait to see whether the gangrene was gone. I had brought the Aerobed® along and was once again staying in Harry's room. Harry was in good spirits during the day, but that night, his leg became increasingly red and hot, and his temperature started rising. I went to tell the nurse, but, incredibly, she was not able to locate any Tylenol to get the fever under control. When she finally decided to go to the hospital pharmacy, I sat helplessly talking to him, stroking his hand. A much older, more seasoned nurse who was just coming off duty came by to see if she could help. By that point, Harry's temperature had spiked over 103. He could barely open his eyes, and he seemed to be lapsing into unconsciousness. The nurse started putting cool wash cloths on his forehead and neck and saying in such a soft, soothing voice,

"Harry? Can you hear me?"

Harry didn't respond, so I started talking to him as well until finally, eyes still closed, he shook his head and said,

"I can't do it this time. This isn't about love anymore."

I was terrified, but the nurse said soothingly,

"Yes, you can. You can do it," and just kept gently wiping his forehead. Taking her lead, I started telling him, too,

"Yes, you can, my loveperson, you can do this," although I didn't know if it was right to ask him to try just this one more time.

"I can't do it," he said again.

Not knowing what else to do, I made my strongest appeal.

"Stay with me," I whispered in tears.

Harry brought my hand up to his lips, kissed it, slowly opened his eyes and said,

"I'll stay with you."

Finally the first nurse came back with the Tylenol, his temperature started to return to normal, and he was all smiles again. When he was finally asleep, I went out in the hallway, sat on the floor, and called my sister, Christie. I didn't know if I had been selfish not to just let him go at that moment, but Christie was certain.

"It wasn't time yet, Eileen. It wasn't his time."

When we hung up, I just sat and cried. He had stayed alive for me. I saw him do it.

The next day, an oncologist came to Harry's room. Oncology was not a topic we were interested in discussing, and no one had told us he would be coming, so we were taken aback. We were cordial, but not encouraging. The oncologist seemed to be just shooting the breeze with us. He didn't allude to any blood work or say anything of any import, so I was a little perplexed about the purpose of his visit. Looking back, I think either he assumed we already understood the gravity of the situation, or he was reluctant to be the one to break the bad news to us. Either way, when he left, my denial was still firmly intact. Nothing he had said made a dent in it.

For the next several days, we were in a holding pattern while Fehring waited to see whether the gangrene was gone. Harry was still in a lot of pain and ate very little. The pain medication made him drowsy, so we spent our days with him sleeping and me reading next to him. Eucharistic ministers still brought us communion for which we were grateful, and Harry always greeted them warmly. He greeted everyone warmly. But I could see something was changing in him. He always smiled at me, and when Fehring came in, Harry would say,

'I love my wife, and I want to get this done and go home with her."

Still, something was changing.

As the July 4th weekend approached, Harry was still in a holding pattern and too weak for therapy. Just getting into a chair was exhausting for him. He encouraged me to go back home for a night or two for a little break. Phaedra came to Charlotte for the weekend, and Harry tried to enlist her help in convincing me saying,

"Phaedra, tell your mother to go home, will you? Tell her I'll be fine, and she needs some rest."

Harry finally convinced me that with Larry and Donna there in Charlotte, he would be fine, that nothing was going to happen anyway. So I drove back down to the lake, and that night, I sat on Harry's pavilion watching fireworks from the boats out on the lake. I felt like I was being tested, but I had no idea what the right answers were. I didn't know what to pray for. How long should we keep fighting? Has he had enough? I couldn't think straight, yet I couldn't stop thinking. Churning.

I got back to Charlotte Sunday at about 11 a.m. Harry was sitting in a chair with a blanket around his legs, head down, and didn't really notice me come in the room. I went and kissed him on the forehead, crouched down by his chair, and took his hand. It was then that he slowly raised his head to look at me, and he took my breath away.

His face was luminous.

"I've been up all night having many, many conversations with God."

"What did you talk about?"

"God asked me if I wanted to live or not," still smiling radiantly.

"What did you tell Him?"

"It took me a lot of time to answer, but I said, 'Yes.' So God said, 'Ok, give it a run. Just like that.'" His face was just shining. Then his eyes got very big, and he said,

"We talked all night. I was sweating. God's big question was, 'Do you have any cojones?'"

"What did you tell Him?"

"I said yes."

So I told Harry about my weekend at the lake, adding,

"We were both wandering in the wilderness this weekend, like Jesus in the desert, and we both decided, 'Yes.'

Harry nodded, so I continued,

"We're going to do this thing we're in - this cross we're carrying together. And do you know who is in this with us?"

Harry's answer gave me a chill.

"Christos."

He answered in the Greek.

In that moment, I knew he was somewhere else. Not on this planet anymore. I can hardly describe to you what happened inside me. Something came crashing down, crash landed. But I smiled at him and asked,

"Yes. Who else?"

"Mary," he smiled.

"Yes. Who else?"

"You and me," eyes sparkling like diamonds.

Yes.

That evening, Fehring's partner was the one making rounds. He stopped in and told us they had concluded that the gangrene was still eating away at Harry's leg. The only option was to amputate the leg just above the knee to get it all. To save Harry's life. He explained this all directly to Harry, and then asked Harry what he wanted to do. Harry told him,

"I love my wife, and I want to stay alive."

They cut off his leg the next morning.

For several more days, they waited to see whether the gangrene was gone. It wasn't. They talked about another amputation which Harry was in favor of, but with me, Fehring seemed annoyed. He had expected me to say, "Okay. We quit," because of whatever the oncologist had privately told him, but I was still confused. No one was being direct with us, and I wanted to support Harry in whichever decision he made - to go through a second amputation or not. After much consternation, Fehring said he would do another amputation only if I signed a "Do Not Resuscitate" order. I was shocked, but still did not have the presence of mind (or the desire) to ask why such an order was even necessary. Denial is like a drug. It floods your system and sets up camp in your mind.

The next morning, Fehring did a second amputation, cutting off more of Harry's leg further up. More days passed in waiting with Fehring becoming more brusque. Now a social worker was brought in, a lovely, empathetic young woman, but I found her just as perplexing as I did everyone else. It seemed to me that all the conversations I had with everyone but Harry were as if we were speaking in two different languages. I would nod, the doctor or social worker would nod, and we would each think we understood the other. In fact, I did not understand a thing they were saying.

One morning, Fehring came in, and while he was taking off the bandaging, launched into a dour description of what he was expecting to see. Once the dressing was off, however, Fehring stopped, stared at Harry's leg for a moment, and said with surprise,

"This actually looks a little better."

Harry beamed broadly and delightedly told Fehring,

"It sounded pretty dark when you first started talking, and then suddenly daisies started sprouting out of your mouth!"

That little bit of progress was enough for them to let us leave the hospital. However, Fehring sent us home with two very confusing, contradictory sets of paperwork. One was for antibiotics and physical therapy. The other was for hospice. I didn't know what to think. I was afraid to hope and afraid not to hope.

Harry had it figured out, though. The morning we left for home, he smiled that luminous smile and told me,

"We're so blessed. We know where God lives."

I wasn't sure what he meant, but I know now.

We lived at a beautiful lake. God lived there, too.

We all lived there together.

"You have no idea how much I love you."
- Harry

~ Harry Has His Way ~

By now you know that Harry died. You saw it coming. July 23, 2008. I didn't know that would be the day he would die, but God knew, and Harry knew, too, at least he knew on that day. There are two things I want to tell you about that day. The first is something I saw right away. The second is something that took me years to see. A true mystic might have understood immediately. Could have done the math.

I wish I could tell you that I used Harry's last days wisely and well. That I lay with him and asked him what was happening. What he saw. But I didn't. I was in such shock, such dogged denial, I wouldn't look at what was really happening. I had emotional blinders on. I was obsessed with the fact that although Fehring had handed us to hospice, he had also ordered antibiotics and physical therapy. How could that be?! I cleaved to that contradiction, clung to that life raft and kept kicking, kept debating that dichotomy with myself and everyone else. It had to be one or the other. So I paced around the house, stayed in constant motion so the truth couldn't pin me down. Couldn't catch me.

The very thing Harry said he did not want to happen was happening.

265

There were so many people there coming and going. Friends, hospice nurses, Harry's son, my daughter, my sister, Christie. Constant chaos. I couldn't understand what was happening, couldn't even get a decent breath in and was hyperventilating all the time. One of the hospice nurses told me, "These are some of the closest times you'll ever have with him," but whenever I was in the bedroom, there was someone else around. I couldn't get a moment alone with him. I wish I had accepted what was happening. I wish I had had the strength to say,

"Everyone go now. It's our time."

I didn't have that kind of strength, but Harry did.

Harry had a plan.

You can stand behind me.

The morning of July 23, Harry's son, John, two hospice nurses, and I were the only people there. We moved Harry onto a hospital bed that we situated right up against the glass doors in our bedroom, so that if Harry opened his eyes, he could see the lake. In mid-afternoon, John said good-bye and headed to the airport to fly back to New York. Harry's daughter, Jennifer, wasn't due to fly in until the next day. The house had been chaotic for days, but now with nearly everyone gone, our home was filled with a quieting calm. I became calm. The quiet gentled the jangling coursing through me. Time started to slow, and I could take a breath. I started to see the wisdom in Harry's wanting to be alone together. The nurses were at Harry's bedside, but when I came into the bedroom, they discretely left and went out into the living room. Our friend Evie had just arrived, but stayed quietly in the doorway. Harry had just been struggling with pain, and the nurses had managed to get some medication down him, so I went over to hold him in my arms until the pain subsided.

That was Harry's moment. Feeling my embrace, Harry slowly roused, looked me squarely in the eyes and said,

"I'm going."

I nodded and choked out,

"I love you."

"I'm going," he said again, still looking in my eyes.

"I love you," I answered again, and I kissed for the last time ever.

That was the last thing Harry heard. He simply closed his eyes and was gone.

I had felt utterly alone in the universe, but the love of my life, seemingly unawares, had chosen that moment for both of us. He could not control his illness, but he could control his death. He always said he wanted to die in my arms with no one else around. With no hysteria. Just a peaceful transition. And he always said I had no idea how much he loved me. He proved his love with his death. Sick as he was, suffering as he was, he somehow held off until we were alone. He saw that window, and that's when he chose to die. In my arms, alone. With that final, heroic act, he was saying,

"You are the only and entire person on the planet that I want with me as I leave."

I was not alone. Harry's love was a shroud over both of us.

Now here's the second thing I want you to understand. Numbers have meaning. Numbers illuminate mysteries of our faith. Twelve tribes, 12 apostles, 40 years wandering the desert, 40 days fasting in the desert.... God uses numbers to show us something significant.

Six were the number of days of creation, signifying completion and symbolizing the principal attributes of God, namely his power, majesty, wisdom, love, mercy, and justice.[1]

Remember my 54 day rosary novena? Twenty-seven days of prayer for a particular petition followed by 27 days of prayer in thanksgiving for the answer to that petition? The last day of petition and the day before Harry and I met was July 23, 2002. Harry died July 23, 2008.

Harry and I had known each other six years to the day.

Completion.

God's healing plan, God's merciful plan, God's loving plan was complete.

1"**NUMBERS, RELIGIOUS.**" Pocket Catholic Dictionary. Abridged edition of *Modern Catholic Dictionary.* New York, New York: Image Books edition published October 1985 by special arrangement with Doubleday.

"Suddenly a light from heaven shined round about him."
- Acts 9:3

~ Omega ~

You might think it ended with the kiss. You'd be wrong. All love comes from God, lives in God. The deepest, fiercest, marrow-deep love of which we are capable is just a glint in the light of God's love.

It started with God's crazy love. And God's love never dies.

I married a convert. A battered prodigal, far from his Father's home. A sailor sunken where the water rocks the slowly drowning swimmer. An errant knight, sheathed and shielded.

Till he tumbled from his horse and was blinded by the light.

This is our love story. Although the events I've told you are ours, this is your love story, too, for one incredible, incomprehensible reason.

God has crazy love for you.

~ Acknowledgments ~

Many people lifted me while I wrote this story. To Mark Molinoff, Penny Juday, and Father Thomas Miles, you each bolstered me at a critical moment. Thank you, David Oh, for teaching me to play the cello and so much more. Thanks to Kathy Sheffield and to my dear Chamber Chicks, Birgid, Liz and Grace, for all their enthusiasm. Thanks also to my patient friends, Cecelia Flanary and Suzy French, who propped me back up when I was listing, and to Keith Flanary and Stu French for proofreading perseveringly. Thanks to Father David Chiantella for reminding me whose book this is, and to Arthur Powers and Ellen Gable Hrkach for helping me take back control. Special thanks to Marguerite Ambrozevitch for championing the book behind the scenes. Thanks to my cousin, Richard Jenkins, who ordered me to barricade myself in my house until I was finished. Thanks to my aunt, Eileen Sorensen, for her constant courage and wisdom, and reminding me, "You have to finish the book. You told me you were going to." Undying thanks to my sister and her husband, Christie and Rob Silbajoris, for giving me a soft spot to land, and to Dave and Evie Kaczkowski for keeping vigil over me and giving me a place where the four of us will always live. Thanks to my sister, Laura Kielmann, who admonished me, "Get out of bed and write, you slacker!" Most of all, my heartfelt thanks to my wonderful sister of the heart, Kay Ruth, who graciously agreed to be my editor and then proved her mettle by giving me a deadline.

~ About the Author ~

Eileen Leamy lives in Raleigh, North Carolina where she teaches RCIA and serves in hospital ministry. Eileen also plays the cello with the Triangle Area Community Orchestra and with her beloved string quartet, The Chamber Chicks.